MASONIC ETIQUETTE
TODAY

A Modern Guide to Masonic Protocol and Practice

by

G.F. Redman, P.G.Swd.B.,
Assistant Grand Secretary

Lewis Masonic

To the Present and Past Grand Secretaries
I have known

First published 2009

ISBN 978 0 85318 297 9

© Graham Redman 2009

Published by Ian Allan Publishing

an imprint of Ian Allan Publishing Ltd, Hersham, Surrey KT12 4RG.
Printed by Ian Allan Printing Ltd, Hersham, Surrey KT12 4RG.

Code: 0909/B

Visit the Ian Allan Publishing website at www.ianallanpublishing.com

Contents

Foreword

For most of us involved in the government of the Craft the first person to whom we turn for authoritative advice on matters of Masonic protocol or the interpretation of the Book of Constitutions is Brother Graham Redman. Over a period of more than twenty years working at a senior level in the Grand Secretary's Office he has accumulated a wealth of experience in matters of Masonic ceremonial, custom and protocol, and in addition he possesses a compendious knowledge – and understanding – of the Book of Constitutions.

Until now the benefit of his accumulated knowledge and wisdom has been readily available only to a small number of us, but by writing this book he has now made it available to the whole Craft. He is too modest to claim or even suggest that the book covers every topic or every situation that can arise, but I do not believe that there has been a more comprehensive work of its kind for very many years, if ever.

Anthony Wilson, PJGW
President, Board of General Purposes

Preface

I

Hot through Troy's ruin Menelaus broke
   To Priam's palace, sword in hand, to sate
   On that adulterous whore a ten years' hate
And a king's honour. Through red death, and smoke,
And cries, and then by quieter ways he strode,
   Till the still innermost chamber fronted him.
   He swung his sword, and crashed into the dim
Luxurious bower, flaming like a god.

High sat white Helen, lonely and serene.
   He had not remembered that she was so fair,
And that her neck curved down in such a way;
And he felt tired. He flung the sword away,
   And kissed her feet, and knelt before her there,
The perfect Knight before the perfect Queen.

II

So far the poet. How should he behold
   That journey home, the long connubial years?
   He does not tell you how white Helen bears
Child on legitimate child, becomes a scold,
Haggard with virtue. Menelaus bold
   Waxed garrulous, and sacked a hundred Troys
   'Twixt noon and supper. And her golden voice
Got shrill as he grew deafer. And both were old.

Often he wonders why on earth he went
   Troyward, or why poor Paris ever came.
Oft she weeps, gummy-eyed and impotent;
   Her dry shanks twitch at Paris' mumbled name.
So Menelaus nagged; and Helen cried;
And Paris slept on by Scamander side.

Rupert Brooke – *Menelaus and Helen*

etiquette 1 the conventional rules of social behaviour. 2 a the customary behaviour of members of a profession towards each other; b the unwritten code governing this.

– Concise Oxford Dictionary

etiquette forms of ceremony or decorum: ceremony: the conventional laws of courtesy observed between members of the same profession, players, etc.

– Chambers Twentieth Century Dictionary

What on earth has a poem by the great English poet Rupert Brooke got to do with Masonic etiquette? Directly, absolutely nothing at all. His poem (which I have quoted in full only after trying unsuccessfully to reduce it to a more manageable-sized bite), however, illustrates rather usefully the way in which etiquette differs from Rules. The first sonnet of Brooke's poem tells the idealised story in high-flown language and magniloquent phrases; the second sonnet tells the story as it was. In the same way the Rules in the Book of Constitutions (and the edicts of the Grand Lodge) in slightly pompous language describe (and prescribe) things as they ought to be; the largely unwritten "rules" of etiquette tell it how it is in practice.

To take a different analogy, the Rules and edicts represent the framework of a building, while etiquette fills in the interstices between the parts of the frame and makes the edifice watertight. Both the poem and the analogy give a much clearer picture of what constitutes *Masonic* etiquette than the two dictionary definitions also quoted at the head of this Preface.

Thirty-five years ago as a new Master Mason I bought and read (I have scarcely opened it since) a book entitled *Freemasonry and its Etiquette* by the impressively named William Preston Campbell-Everden.[1] Judging by his name, his parents had clearly destined him for great things in a Masonic career. It is true that he succeeded in gaining the Emulation silver matchbox for working the Ceremony

---

1. His book is advertised on its title page as incorporating *The Etiquette of Freemasonry* By "An Old Past Master" – rather like a Victorian book of social etiquette By A Lady of Title (probably a title of such obscurity that it would cut little ice with potential purchasers of her book, being known only to those in her immediate circle – from whom she was, no doubt, anxious to conceal the fact that her income was so meagre that she was reduced to supplementing it by writing such a book).

of Installation in 1914 without standing in need of prompting or correction, but on the evidence of that book his parents' ambitions remained largely unfulfilled.

He defined etiquette in part as "the minor jurisprudence of Freemasonry". His book quoted or paraphrased large chunks of the Book of Constitutions, a proceeding on which I looked with disfavour when I started to write this book, but with which I began to have much more sympathy as I wrote more and more of it. For the truth is, following the analogy given above, that to understand how etiquette fills in the gaps in the framework it is necessary to have a clear understanding of the framework itself. I therefore make no apology for the fact that much of what follows amounts to a commentary on the relevant part of the Book of Constitutions, supplemented by various edicts of the Grand Lodge and rulings by the Board of General Purposes and others, and interspersed with a discussion of the relevant etiquette.

I have tried to make the book comprehensive, so that there is advice in it for the new Master Mason, but also guidance for those Brethren who are very much his seniors in years and rank. I am conscious that in doing so I have laid myself open to the charge of talking at times over the head of the former, but I console myself with the thought that as he progresses in the Craft he will be able to return to this book time after time for guidance as he reaches each new level in his Masonic career, until he is finally numbered among the latter.

Masonic etiquette, like social etiquette, is generally a matter of good manners and good behaviour. As such, therefore, it is not just a matter of keeping within the Law or the Rules; it is a matter of doing what is "good form" over and above what falls within the Law or the Rules. It is also worth remembering that "good form" is also sometimes dependent on the context and on what other people are doing. Most of the instances of "bad form" that occur are the result of not knowing what is the right thing to do, not a deliberate flouting of the conventions (though some, alas, are).

For those who wish to find their way through the maze of what is lawful, what is correct and, not least, what is proper, this book is written. I cannot claim that it is definitive, because etiquette is in a constant state of change. What is more, as I write this Preface I am left with a feeling that it is only "work in progress", since hardly a day has gone by in recent months when I have not felt that yet another topic which has come across my desk deserves to be covered in it.

* * * * *

There are very many Brethren who in one way or another have, directly or indirectly, given me help or encouragement in the preparation and writing of this book. Some of them have answered (or in some cases – and no less importantly – asked) no more than a single question. They are, alas, too numerous for me to mention all but a few by name.

I must first thank the Board of General Purposes for giving me permission to quote from the Proceedings of the Grand Lodge, the Book of Constitutions and other official publications of the United Grand Lodge of England, as well as from material produced by me in my capacity as Assistant Grand Secretary on matters within the public domain; while these source materials themselves may be regarded as authoritative, not every conclusion drawn from them or every opinion that I have expressed should necessarily be regarded as representing the view of the Grand Lodge or the Board. I am also grateful to my colleagues at Freemasons' Hall and, in particular, W Bro. Andrew Croci, Head of the Registration Section, who has read most of this book in draft form and has made many constructive comments of which I have been glad to take note. Finally, I am especially grateful to RW Bro. Anthony Wilson, PJGW, President of the Board of General Purposes, for agreeing to contribute a Foreword to this book.

Graham Redman
April 2009

Part I

INSIDE THE LODGE

1

DRESS

DRESS AT MASONIC MEETINGS

Brethren will no doubt have noticed that instructions for Masonic functions held under the auspices of Grand Lodge indicate that dark clothing, black tie and white collar should be worn. The Board strongly recommends to Masters of Lodges, on whom the final responsibility must rest, that they should by example and encouragement lead their members to a standard of dress compatible with the dignity of the Order.

It is felt that, with the end of clothes rationing, it is not unreasonable to hope that dark suits, black shoes and ties, and white collars will become the general wear with Masonic clothing.

Extract from the Report of the Board of
General Purposes, adopted June 1950

From time to time the Board of General Purposes has given guidance on the standards of dress to be observed by members of the Craft, either in its Reports to the Grand Lodge or in letters issued on its behalf by the Grand Secretary. The guidance has been aimed at ensuring that a suitable level of smartness is maintained, coupled with a measure of uniformity that nevertheless avoids suppressing all scope for individuality.

Over the last hundred years the clothes that Brethren have been expected to wear to Lodge meetings have changed significantly, but the underlying criteria have hardly changed at all. These remain a dark coat (or jacket) and trousers, a white shirt (or at least a white collar), black shoes and an appropriate tie. This was typically exemplified until the Second World War by evening dress (either white tie and tails, or black tie and dinner jacket), during the Second World War by morning dress (the result of a combination of the blackout and rationing), and since the war by a full range from one end of the spectrum to the other.

Thus before the Second World War one of my Lodges used to meet in dinner jackets, but in white tie and tails for the Installation. During the war it met, in common with most other Lodges, during the daytime, and therefore the members wore morning dress, typically black jacket and waistcoat with striped trousers, and substituting an ordinary black tie for a black or white bow tie. Also, in common with other Lodges, it abandoned the wearing of white gloves, which required precious clothing coupons. After the War, when meetings moved back to the evening, morning dress was retained, though with dinner jackets resumed for the Installation. At some point before I joined it in the late 1970s dinner jackets had been abandoned altogether and many Brethren were already wearing a dark lounge suit. At the time of writing, a lounge suit is so much the norm that a black jacket with striped trousers, once virtually *de rigueur* for Grand Officers, looks decidedly out of place.

Indeed, an interesting inversion is now discernible, in that those Brethren for whom a lounge suit is no longer a standard item in their wardrobe, but who in earlier times would have bought a lounge suit for Lodge meetings, have recently taken instead to buying a black jacket and striped trousers for Lodge meetings.

What I have written above may seem rather discursive, but it illustrates several points: first, that Masonic etiquette or practice, like any form of etiquette, is not static but is in a constant state of change; secondly, that the Grand Lodge, for all that it is often perceived as being dictatorial or prescriptive, applies a fairly light touch in relation to things that do not involve matters of serious principle; and thirdly, that a dress code and its evolution, like many other things, is very much a matter for individual Lodges.

It goes – or should go – without saying that a member of a Lodge should be careful to conform to the dress code it has adopted. A visitor also should, as a part of the courtesy that is one of the reciprocal obligations of hospitality, conform if he is able – and if he is not, should at least show sensitivity – to the customs of his hosts (see also Chapter 7).

There is still a wide range of different dress styles in the many Lodges of the English Constitution. At one end of the spectrum, the Officers (other than the Stewards) of Apollo University Lodge, No. 357 (Oxford) wear court dress (*i.e.* knee breeches, black silk stockings and buckled shoes, white tie and waistcoat with an evening tail-coat) to its meetings, while the other Brethren generally wear dinner jackets (or uniform). In Isaac Newton University Lodge, No. 859 (Cambridge) the Officers (other than the Stewards) wear court dress (with a Cambridge blue garter on the left leg, and a black waistcoat), the Stewards and other members wear dinner jackets, and Grand Officers wear morning dress. In Foxhunters Lodge, No. 3094 (London) the members wear evening dress, with a Hunt Coat, usually pink (*i.e.* scarlet). Many Lodges still meet in dinner jackets, either at the Installation alone or at all meetings. For most, however, morning dress – either black jacket with striped trousers,[1] or a dark lounge suit – has now become the rule, though in a few of those Lodges Officers are expected to wear a morning coat. Properly, a waistcoat[2] (black) should be worn not only with a morning coat but also with black jacket and striped trousers, unless the jacket is a double-breasted one, when the waistcoat is customarily dispensed with; but there is a discernible trend away from this, assimilating a single-breasted black jacket and striped trousers to a two-piece lounge suit.

Although the Board of General Purposes has recently (December 2002) reaffirmed that unless it is the custom of a Lodge to meet in evening dress, traditional morning wear or dark lounge suit continues to be the appropriate dress, there are two further possibilities that are met with from time to time: uniform and Highland dress. The first is unexceptionable, as it has a long and honourable tradition in English Craft Masonry, and may take the form of mess kit for evening dress or full uniform for morning dress. Historically, it has been an option for regimental Lodges or for serving members of the armed forces, but is nowadays almost entirely confined to the former situation. Highland dress is more controversial. In some (though limited) circumstances it may be an instance of military uniform, but otherwise many would hold that the wearing of the kilt should be confined to the Highlands. I cannot recall any occasion when I have seen any of the most senior Grand Officers of the Grand Lodge of Scotland attend a Lodge meeting in England wearing Highland dress. There are, however, several Lodges in Provinces, founded for expatriate Scots or those of Scots descent, which have sought and received their Provincial Grand Master's blessing to meeting in Highland dress. This is, perhaps, in itself harmless, but some of the members of such Lodges appear to feel themselves licensed to wear Highland dress when visiting other Lodges, in disregard of the dress codes of the latter (see also Chapter 7).

In the Grand Lodge, where more formal standards naturally apply, the dress for English Constitution Brethren is unashamedly morning dress, with present Grand

---

1 The traditional alternative to stripes of "shepherd's check" is now virtually never met with.

2 It is a quirk of sartorial fashion that while a straight-bottomed waistcoat is worn with all the buttons fastened, a waistcoat of the more common pattern, with two points at the bottom, is worn with the last button left undone.

Officers wearing a black morning coat and past Grand Officers generally wearing a black jacket – in each case with black waistcoat and striped trousers – with many of the other Brethren following their example. In Metropolitan, Provincial and District Grand Lodges much the same "rules" apply, though with wide local variations, so that, for example, in some Provinces all Grand Officers, from the Provincial Grand Master down, wear a black jacket rather than a morning coat, while in others all Grand Officers, present or past, and the "key" Provincial Grand Officers are expected as a matter of course to wear a morning coat.

All Brethren are expected to wear a white collar (and the Grand Director of Ceremonies and his Deputies have traditionally imposed upon themselves the standard of a stiff detachable white collar) and though a shirt itself need not necessarily be white, it is expected in every case to be of a restrained stripe pattern or hue (see *Information for the Guidance of Members of the Craft* – "Standard of Dress").

Ties have long been a vexed question. It is unlikely that any problem will arise in relation to evening dress, where the length of the coat will dictate whether a black (or Craft) bow tie or a white bow tie is to be worn. Similarly, in the Grand Lodge the Craft tie or a plain black tie (other than the Craft tie, a tie bearing an emblem, whether in the weave or as a coloured design, is not acceptable), is prescriptive. Where, however, morning dress in any of its variants is worn in a Private Lodge the position is far more complex and some knowledge or understanding of the relevant local practice is essential.

The starting point must always be a plain black tie or the Craft tie. An absolute "don't" is any tie that is directly associated with an Order other than the Craft or Royal Arch: the only Masonic ties that may be worn are those with a specific Craft or Royal Arch connotation, and not even all of those are acceptable.

Many Provinces now have special ties, which members of the Province concerned are encouraged to wear in Provincial Grand Lodge and Lodges within the Province. The same is the case in the Metropolitan Area of London and in many Districts. The Board of General Purposes has now made it clear that such ties may be worn within the particular Metropolitan Area, Province or District to which they relate, but that they should not be worn when visiting a Lodge in another Metropolitan Area, Province or District unless that Metropolitan, Provincial or District Grand Master has given his permission (see again *Information for the Guidance of Members of the Craft* – "Standard of Dress"). A visitor, moreover, should not simply assume that such permission has been given, but should take steps to assure himself that it has. As a matter of etiquette, the permission of the relevant Masonic authority should not be taken as a licence to wear whichever of his Metropolitan, Provincial or District ties a Brother chooses; someone who *belongs to* a Lodge in Surrey and a Lodge in Middlesex might properly wear either of those Provincial ties if visiting a Lodge in London, but it would *not* be appropriate for him to wear his Surrey tie in Middlesex or vice versa, even if he is a visitor to the Lodge he is attending.

By established custom, Regimental, College or School, Hospital, Livery and similar ties have come to be worn in Lodges associated with the regiment etc to which they relate. The Board has now affirmed that these may continue to be worn in such circumstances. Convention plays a part here also: various more or less formal groupings of Lodges have grown up over the years, and with them the custom of wearing the appropriate tie in the other Lodges in the particular group. Thus Regimental ties may be worn in other Regimental Lodges, Livery ties in other Livery Lodges and so on; but it is wrong in principle to wear a Livery tie in a Regimental Lodge or a School tie in a Hospital Lodge. There are even further subtleties involved. Not every Lodge with such a connection has chosen to wear the relevant tie, so that a visitor from a similar Lodge should not automatically assume that his Regimental, College, School, Hospital or Livery tie is appropriate wear. Similarly there exist two separate groupings of old school Lodges: the Public School Lodges' Council and the Federation of School Lodges (of which the latter is much the larger). It used to be a convention – less scrupulously observed now than formerly – that a member of one of the Lodges in one grouping did not wear his School tie when visiting a Lodge in the other grouping.

Finally, the Board of General Purposes has never shown any enthusiasm at all for any Masonic tie the wearing of which is confined to the members of a particular Lodge. Such a tie is essentially divisive and is almost certainly unnecessary, as it cannot be worn in any Lodge other than that to which it relates (see above) whose members ought to be able to identify each other without recourse to a special tie. It differs from the Regimental and similar ties just discussed in that they are capable of being worn by many individuals besides the members of the Lodge, so that they mark the overlap between the Craft and another organisation or group, whereas a Lodge tie is confined to members of the Craft alone.

2

REGALIA

239. The regalia, clothing, insignia and jewels to be worn are as hereinafter prescribed, and no Brother shall be admitted into any meeting of the Grand Lodge, or of any subordinate Lodge, without the clothing appropriate to his rank under the Grand Lodge.

Rule 239, Book of Constitutions

With the exception of Masonic rank – particularly Grand Rank – which is in a class of its own, there can scarcely be a topic more emotive or that gives rise to greater heartache, irritation, misunderstanding and sometimes deliberate misbehaviour than that of regalia. The disdain that many Masons profess for elaboration in regalia is not borne out in practice in their enthusiasm for appearing in all the finery they are allowed to wear – and even in some which they are not. Even so, for every Brother who sets out to disobey the Rules on regalia, there are very many more who do so through ignorance or misunderstanding, or because they have received the wrong advice from those who might be supposed to know, but who have themselves fallen into error. Perhaps the way in which the Rules relating to regalia in the Book of Constitutions are laid out is partly to blame, in that, except for the description of the aprons in Rule 265, they start with the highest ranks and work downwards, so that the Rules relating to ordinary Brethren are tucked away at the end of each section, whereas every Freemason starts his Masonic career at the bottom and works his way upwards.

Aprons and collars
The distinguishing badge of every Mason is the apron, the various gradations of which are set out in Rule 265. Every Mason wears the same basic apron of white lambskin, which becomes increasingly elaborately ornamented as he progresses through his Masonic career. The apron is not only the distinguishing badge of a

Mason, it is also a badge of distinction; as such, even though it may be old, and even faded with the passage of time, it should be worn with pride and decorum. The aprons of an Entered Apprentice and a Fellow Craft are generally secured with tapes or "strings", and can easily be tied firmly round the waist; most others are secured with a belt with a traditional snake fastening, and if the belt is not sufficiently tightened the apron will sag in an unsightly manner, which looks anything but smart. The aprons of some of the most senior Grand Officers are fitted with a becket, a small loop of dark blue material which is passed over the middle button of the Brother's jacket or morning coat, thus supporting some of the weight of the heavily embroidered apron, and ensuring that it hangs smartly. If a morning coat is worn, the belt of the apron should be above, and therefore supported by, the two buttons on the back of the coat, thus preventing the coat from riding up in an unsightly manner. I mention this because it gives an indication of the height at which the apron should be worn. In the English Constitution, unlike the Irish and the Scottish, the apron is worn over the coat or jacket, except with an evening tail-coat, when it is worn under the coat. In some Workings the flap of the Entered Apprentice's apron is expected to be worn turned up, but in most the flap is turned down like those of all other aprons.

For an Entered Apprentice a plain white apron is normally the only regalia he wears. For many Brethren, however, it is not long before appointment to office brings with it a collar and jewel. The collars of the Officers of Private Lodges are of light blue ribbon, with a button and double cord of silver where the collar comes to a point (similar, except for the colour, to the collar of a Grand Officer illustrated in Plate 51 of the Appendix to the Book of Constitutions). There are only four Lodges for which an exception to this pattern is authorised by the Book of Constitutions: The Grand Stewards' Lodge, whose Officers' and Past Masters' collars are of red, and the three Time Immemorial Lodges (Lodge of Antiquity, No. 2; Royal Somerset House and Inverness Lodge, No. 4; and Lodge of Fortitude and Old Cumberland, No. 12) whose Officers' and Past Masters' collars have a garter-blue stripe of one third of the collar's width in the centre. Officers' collars may be worn *only* in the Lodge to which they relate, except those of the Master and his two Wardens, which *must* also be worn in the Grand Lodge and the relevant (but no other) Metropolitan, Provincial or District Grand Lodge; *even they may be worn nowhere else*, except on a special occasion when ordered by the Grand Master. An Officer's collar may additionally be ornamented with a chain, which must be fastened over the centre of the collar (Rule 262), but relatively few Lodges have such chains on the Master's collar and far fewer have them on the collars of the other Officers. The design of any such chain requires the approval of the Grand Master, though if one of the standard patterns is adopted, approval is needed only for some special feature, such as the inclusion of the Lodge's badge in the design.

The light blue Master Mason's or Installed Master's apron of a present Officer of a Private Lodge may be ornamented with the emblem of his office in silver (or white) within a double circle, usually bearing the name and number of the Lodge. Such aprons, unlike Officers' collars, are not required by Rule 265 to be worn only in the Lodge to which they relate, but in practice the Master's apron is the only one commonly to be met with elsewhere. Quite apart from the fact that, as a matter of etiquette, it is "bad form" for a more junior Officer to wear an apron showing his office, other than in the Lodge to which it relates, Lodges themselves are generally extremely reluctant to allow junior Brethren to take away expensive embroidered aprons to show off elsewhere. No such ambiguity applies to the light blue Officers' gauntlets, which may be worn *only* in the Lodge to which they relate. The only other ornament permitted by Rule 265 to a "light blue" apron is the three-quarter-inch wide garter-blue stripe on the inner edge of the border of the aprons of members of the Prince of Wales's Lodge, No. 259. By long custom, however, a few Lodges continue to wear non-standard regalia: thus, the members of Middlesex Lodge, No. 143 (London) wear aprons with a light blue border three and a half inches wide with a silver cord on the inner edge, while the Officers of the Lodge of Fortitude, No. 64 (East Lancashire) have aprons ornamented with silver lace on both the outer and inner edges of the light blue border.

A Brother standing in for an Officer of a Lodge who is absent should wear the collar and jewel of that office, even if he is a visitor; but if the Officer is present, the stand-in must not take over his collar, but be dressed according to his own rank or office.

A Brother who has served for a full year as Master of a Lodge and has vacated the Chair on the installation of his successor is not only entitled to, but must, wear the collar and jewel of a Past Master at all Craft meetings – until he is able to exchange it for one of a higher rank: it is as much a part of his essential regalia as his apron, or the collar and jewel of a Provincial or District Grand Officer or holder of a London (Metropolitan) or Overseas Rank. Such collars, except for those of the Past Masters of the four Lodges mentioned above in relation to Officers' collars, are of light blue, and all except those of The Grand Stewards' Lodge have a central braid of silver. If a Past Master holds an office in his Lodge he must wear the Officer's collar over his Past Master's collar. A Brother who has resigned from his Lodge during his year in the Chair (which is the only way he can resign as Master) is not entitled to wear a Past Master's collar as he has not completed a full year in the Chair; he will in consequence be a trap for the Directors of Ceremonies of Lodges he visits, as it will be impossible, without inside knowledge, to distinguish him from a current Master of a Lodge.

Thus far the position is relatively straightforward, though Brethren do still make mistakes, the most common being the wearing of his Master's collar by a Master of one Private Lodge visiting another – generally the result of the Master having been encouraged to take his collar away with him so that he may represent his Lodge in the Grand Lodge or the Metropolitan, Provincial or District Grand Lodge.

From here on, however, questions of protocol are both more frequent and more complex. Every Provincial or District Grand Officer (other than a Steward), and every holder of a Metropolitan or Overseas Rank, has a choice between dress (or "full dress") and undress regalia. Interestingly, although the expressions "dress regalia" and "undress regalia" are used very widely by members of the Craft, from the lowest to the very highest level, neither is to be found in the Book of Constitutions, which adopts a more cumbersome mode of description. Dress regalia is ornamented with gold lace (while the apron has a gold fringe and the embroidered emblem and "levels" are in gilt); undress regalia is ornamented with gold cord (while the apron has no fringe, and the embroidery and "levels" are in garter-blue). To be even more precise, the Rules in the Book of Constitutions provide that those who hold these offices or ranks *may* wear such regalia at all meetings (though they may claim precedence only within the area to which the office or rank relates), the implication being that they may, if they wish, wear the light blue regalia of a Past Master or Master Mason as the case may be. [1] It is not, however, common to see such Brethren exercising their right to wear light blue! [2] It is not uncommon for a Brother who belongs to Lodges in more than one Province (or London) to hold Provincial Grand Rank in each. It is always tempting to such a Brother to wear the regalia of the highest rank he holds, but as those ranks carry no precedence outside the Province concerned (see above), it is only proper, as well as a kindness to Directors of Ceremonies, to wear the regalia appropriate to the Province in which the Lodge he is attending is situated.

---

1 See Rule 239, quoted at the head of this chapter – "rank under the *Grand* Lodge"

2 Indeed, it was for some years a grievance of holders of London Rank (the name by which London Grand Rank was known until 1939) that they were obliged to attend the Grand Lodge wearing their Past Masters' collars.

According to Rule 260 of the Book of Constitutions, the decision whether to wear dress or undress regalia is one for the free choice of the individual wearer. In practice – and this is where etiquette comes in – unless the usage of a particular Lodge is otherwise, the holders of these ranks usually wear undress, but bring out their dress regalia both on those occasions when a Grand Officer would be expected to wear his dress regalia and at Lodge Installations. Some Brethren for reasons of economy, or because they rarely attend meetings other than those of their mother Lodge, buy only one set or the other – quite often full dress. It is certainly best that such a Brother wears dress regalia on the occasion of his investiture with his new rank, and if his financial circumstances are such that he can only afford undress regalia (the former custom in some Lodges of making a present of his regalia to a newly promoted Brother being all but dead), it is to be hoped that some Brother will lend him the appropriate full dress for the occasion.

At the risk of being repetitive, but for the avoidance of doubt, a Provincial or District Grand Officer (or holder of a Metropolitan or Overseas Rank) who is in office in his Lodge must wear his dark blue collar beneath his Officer's collar. Strongly to be deprecated, however, is the practice (less common nowadays, I am glad to be able to record, than formerly) of folding the point of the collar backwards underneath itself so that the jewel suspended from it hangs through the "v" of the Officer's collar. The reason generally given by those who adopt this practice is that it prevents the two jewels from rattling against each other, the prominent display of the jewel of rank being an entirely unintended consequence!

Metropolitan, Provincial or District Grand Stewards have only one apron and collar, the apron being edged with crimson ribbon, with the emblem of office as well as the "levels" also in crimson, and the collar being of ribbon two and a half inches wide instead of the usual four inches. A Past Provincial or District Grand Steward is distinguished from a present holder of the office by a silver braid in the centre of the collar, similar to the braid on a Past Master's collar. Whereas, however, Provincial and District Grand Stewards, both present and past, wear their regalia at all meetings (until, of course, they are promoted to a higher rank), present Metropolitan Grand Stewards (who are automatically holders of London Grand Rank) wear their aprons and collars only when ordered by the Metropolitan Grand Master to appear in an official capacity; there is, at any rate at present, no apron or collar permitted by the Book of Constitutions for a past Metropolitan Grand Steward.

Just to complicate matters even more, when attending the Grand Lodge a Provincial or District Grand Officer, or holder of London or Overseas Grand Rank, may wear the collar appropriate to the office or rank "in right of which he is attending" – Rule 260(iv).

As might be expected, the position is even more complicated for the Brother who becomes a Grand Officer. Leaving the Grand Stewards aside for the present, Grand Officers, like their Metropolitan, Provincial or District counterparts, have a choice between dress and undress regalia. Their aprons are more elaborate than those of the latter, and their dress collars are edged with gold lace and heavily embroidered in gold with an ear of corn and sprig of acacia. Except when required by the Rules to wear a chain, a present or past Grand Officer has more or less a free choice between dress and undress regalia. Most Grand Officers buy both dress and undress, since it is in the nature of things that they are likely to attend more meetings than holders of Provincial or District ranks, while the sheer cost of dress regalia means that they will not wish to wear it on "everyday" occasions. Whereas, however, he generally has a free choice, a Grand Officer is to wear dress regalia, unless it is impracticable, in the Grand Lodge, at great Ceremonials and Consecrations, and on other special occasions authorised by the Grand Master, as well as in any Metropolitan, Provincial or District Grand Lodge when desired by the Metropolitan, Provincial or District Grand Master.

Chains

Whenever a Grand Officer, other than a Metropolitan, Provincial or District Grand Master or a Grand Inspector, wears a Grand Officer's chain, he must wear a dress apron, the apron being that to which the chain relates. In this context "Grand Officer" means not only a present Grand Officer, but also a Past Grand Officer "recalled to the colours" as a stand-in for a present Grand Officer who is unavailable. Grand Officers wear chains in the Grand Lodge and when ordered by the Grand Master to appear in an *official* capacity. Thus those Grand Officers (present or past) taking an active part in a Consecration wear chains (but not those Grand Officers of the year who happen merely to be attending). By way of contrast, it is the current practice that at the Installation of a new Provincial Grand Master chains are worn not only by those Grand Officers (present or past) taking an active part but also by other Grand Officers of the year (but not past Grand Officers) who are present; the latter are deemed to be carrying out the functions of their office by attending, and they are invariably included in the Installing Officer's procession, which nowadays includes (but did not until recently do so) also those Grand Officers of the year who are members of the host

Province, except for those taking part in the meeting in their capacity as acting Provincial Grand Officers. The same practice is adopted when a Ruler attends an ordinary meeting of a Metropolitan, Provincial or District Grand Lodge.

There is also a general authority given to certain "executive" Grand Officers to wear chains on those occasions when, unless it is impracticable, a Grand Officer is to wear dress regalia (see above); it is considered that these attend such meetings in an official, rather than a private, capacity. The list of "executive" Grand Officers has been slightly expanded over the years, and comprises, broadly speaking, those who would normally be expected to hold their Offices for at least three years.

Slightly different rules have always applied when a present or past Grand Officer attends a meeting of *another* Grand Lodge in a representative capacity, but as this book is concerned with the protocol that applies within the English Constitution, and as such Brethren will invariably be given explicit instructions for the particular occasion, it is not necessary to elaborate on them here.

The most senior Officers of a Metropolitan, Provincial or District Grand Lodge, as well as Grand Inspectors, are also required to wear chains on certain occasions (and for that reason are often referred to colloquially as "Chains"). Here it can be difficult to navigate successfully round the various Rules that apply. On those occasions when a Grand Officer is required to wear dress regalia, unless it is impracticable, such senior Officers – including the Metropolitan, Provincial or District Grand Master (Rule 255) – *must* wear their chains (Rule 256). They must also wear their chains when *officially* present at any Lodge of their respective Metropolitan Area, Province or District (or, in the case of a Grand Inspector, Group). On all other occasions, subject to one exception (see below), they *must* wear collars (Rules 257 and 260).

The effect of these Rules was largely disregarded for many years in a significant number of Provinces, with chains being worn in Private Lodges outside the Province to which they related. As a result, in its Report to the Grand Lodge in December 2006, the Board of General Purposes drew attention to the "measure of misunderstanding of the Rules in the Book of Constitutions relating to the occasions on which chains may be worn". After summarising the effect of the relevant Rules, the Report continued:

> "The Board is of the opinion that on major ceremonial occasions, including meetings of Grand Lodge and Metropolitan, Provincial and District Grand Lodges, a chain indicates the *status* of its wearer within the Craft as a whole, whereas the wearing of a chain on an ordinary

occasion in a Private Lodge is an assertion of the *authority* over that Lodge of the Brother who wears it. It therefore follows that only a Brother who is entitled to preside in a Lodge in accordance with Rule 122 of the Book of Constitutions may properly wear a chain. The Board is, however, aware that it is not uncommon for a Provincial Grand Master, if aware that another Provincial Grand Master (or a Deputy or Assistant Provincial Grand Master) is due to visit a Lodge of his Province, to issue an invitation to the visitor to wear his chain, perhaps in the belief that this is a pleasant courtesy between Provinces.

"The Board, for the reason already given, is in no doubt that the practice, however well intentioned, is based on a fundamental misunderstanding of the significance to be attached to the wearing of a chain. Moreover, in view of the mandatory wording of Rules 257 and 260, no Brother, however senior, has the power to override those Rules and grant what is sometimes mistakenly referred to as a 'dispensation' to another to wear a chain when the Rules clearly require him to wear a collar.

"It also happens from time to time that a Lodge meets by dispensation at a venue that falls within a different Province from that to which the Lodge belongs. By granting the dispensation the Provincial Grand Master having jurisdiction over the particular location has ceded his rights over it, and it has thereupon become temporarily a part of the Province to which the Lodge belongs. He is therefore not entitled to wear his chain if he attends that Lodge, which although meeting *in* his Province is not a Lodge *of* his Province within the scope of Rules 255 and 256."

This clarification of the position was not universally well received, notably (and perhaps understandably) in those Provinces where the Rules had long been ignored or misunderstood. As a result of representations, an amendment to Rule 255 was introduced in June 2007, which provided that a Metropolitan, Provincial or District Grand Master may also wear a chain, if invited to do so by the local Metropolitan, Provincial or District Grand Master, when visiting a Lodge of the latter's Metropolitan Area, Province or District, at which the latter is required (or would be required if he were present) to wear a chain. The amendment did not extend to Deputy and Assistant Metropolitan, Provincial or District Grand Masters, and even in the case of a Metropolitan, Provincial or District Grand

Master himself it is dependent on an invitation from the host Metropolitan, Provincial or District Grand Master.

As a basic rule, when a Grand Officer wears a Grand Officer's chain, he wears a black morning coat (*i.e.* tail-coat) with it. He also wears the dress apron to which the chain relates. [3] If a Grand Officer, present or past, wears a collar, he wears it with a morning (short black) jacket or a lounge suit; this is the case whether full dress or undress regalia is worn. This is, however, no more than a basic rule, and on some occasions different principles may apply. Local practice as to the wearing of a tail-coat often varies from one Province or District to another. At the annual meeting of many Provincial Grand Lodges, all Grand Officers, since they are wearing full dress regalia, are expected to wear a morning coat with it. But there are notable exceptions, so that in at least two Provinces in East Anglia short black jackets, rather than morning coats, are worn by all those attending, from the Provincial Grand Master downwards.

There is a similar variation in practice at meetings of Private Lodges, the hierarchy of some Provinces habitually turning out in morning coats if wearing chains (in such cases almost invariably with a full dress apron), whereas in others a Provincial chain is generally worn with a short black jacket. When officially present at a private Lodge of his Metropolitan Area, Province or District, a Metropolitan, Provincial or District Grand Master is permitted to wear his chain with his undress apron (Rule 266); this, it should be noted, is the *only* situation in which a Grand Officer is permitted to wear a *Grand Officer's* chain with an undress apron. A Deputy or Assistant Metropolitan, Provincial or District Grand Master, or a Metropolitan Grand Inspector, who is a Grand Officer may wear his chain with his Grand Officer's apron (Rule 267), either dress or undress. However, a Deputy or Assistant Metropolitan, Provincial or District Grand Master, or a Metropolitan Grand Inspector, who is not a Grand Officer, should always wear his dress Metropolitan, Provincial or District apron if he wears his chain.

Conflicts between office and rank

Although the effect of Rule 239 is to require that Grand Officers, like other Brethren, must be clothed according to their rank, by virtue of Rule 267 a Grand

---

3   Incidentally, the dress aprons in the Grand Lodge's own set for the use of the present Grand Officers have no tassels – almost certainly a reflection of the fashion prevailing at the time the set was originally purchased, which has been perpetuated as the aprons have been replaced or renewed piecemeal.

Officer who is performing official duties as a present Metropolitan, Provincial or District Grand Officer may (but need not) wear his Metropolitan, Provincial or District collar with his Grand Officer's apron. It follows from this that such a Grand Officer has three options: he may wear only his regalia as a Grand Officer; he may take advantage of Rule 267 and wear his Metropolitan, Provincial or District Grand Officer's collar in substitution for that of a Grand Officer; or, more unusually, he may wear his Metropolitan, Provincial or District collar, on top of his Grand Officer's collar. The choice is, however, only open to him when he is performing *official duties*, so that, for example, if he is attending his own Lodge in the normal way, or visiting another as a private guest, he must not wear his Metropolitan, Provincial or District collar and jewel. This is, perhaps, a convenient point at which to note the effect of Rule 254, which provides: "In every case there shall be appended to the chain or collar the jewel appropriate to the office or rank to which such chain or collar relates, and no other." Although it is an undoubted breach of the Rule, one does occasionally see a Grand Officer improperly wearing on his *Grand Officer's* collar the jewel of a Provincial Office that he holds.

An analogous situation arises when a present Grand Officer, for example (at the time of writing) the President of the Board of General Purposes or the Assistant Grand Secretary, has a higher personal rank than the office which he holds. In the Grand Lodge or elsewhere, when wearing a chain, there will be no difficulty, since he *must* wear the dress apron to which the chain relates. On other occasions, whether with dress or undress regalia, he may wear (a) the apron, collar and jewel of his personal rank, or (b) the apron, collar and jewel of his present office, or (c) the apron of his personal rank, with the collar and jewel of his office. All three options are legitimate, and which is chosen will depend upon the personal preference of the individual Grand Officer. The late RW Bro. Sir Sydney White used always to wear his Grand Secretary's regalia, on the ground that many Brethren were entitled to dress as Past Junior Grand Wardens, but only one as Grand Secretary. Other Grand Secretaries since, once promoted to the higher rank, have opted for a Junior Grand Warden's apron with the Grand Secretary's collar and jewel. In the same way, a present Provincial or District Grand Officer who is not also a Grand Officer, if he holds a personal rank higher than his office, has a similiar choice.

Grand Stewards – red regalia

A Grand Steward (like his Metropolitan, Provincial or District counterpart – see above – but unlike the other Grand Officers) has only one set of regalia to wear, namely an apron with a broad edging of crimson, but *no* emblem on it, and a collar of crimson ribbon four inches wide. The latter has a button and double cord of silver; the collar of a Past Grand Steward is similar, but has an edging of silver cord similar to the gold cord edging on a Provincial or District Grand Officer's undress collar.[4]

This is an appropriate point at which to deal with the wearing of red regalia generally. Despite the clear wording of Rule 239 quoted at the head of this chapter, by very long-standing custom the members of The Grand Stewards' Lodge who are Grand Officers attend its meetings wearing their regalia as present or past Grand Stewards, rather than their Grand Officers' dark blue. As we have already seen, the collars of the Officers and Past Masters of The Grand Stewards' Lodge are of crimson ribbon, rather than of light blue. By analogy, though with nothing like the same length of tradition to support the practice, members of Provincial and District Grand Stewards' Lodges, most of whom have a higher (sometimes much higher) rank than Past Provincial or District Grand Steward, generally attend the meetings of such Lodges wearing a Past Provincial or District Grand Steward's regalia. Some at least of these Lodges have sought to extend to themselves the special privilege granted to The Grand Stewards' Lodge, by clothing their Officers in narrow crimson collars similar to those of Provincial or District Grand Stewards. There is nothing in the Rules of the Book of Constitutions to authorise or justify this practice, but it has been permitted to continue for many years, with Masonic authority turning a blind eye to it. There is, however, at least one exception to this: a Provincial Grand Stewards' Lodge consecrated some twenty-five years ago in the presence of a number of distinguished visitors, including the then Master of The Grand Stewards' Lodge, chose to provide its Officers with four-inch-wide crimson collars. It thereby attracted the wrath of the Board of General Purposes (on the complaint of The Grand Stewards' Lodge, whose special privilege was thereby being infringed) and as a consequence the Lodge was left in no doubt that it must abide by the strict requirements of Rule 262; its Officers, therefore, wear the light blue collars prescribed by the Rule.

---

4 As an exception, a Past Grand Steward who is the Master or a Past Master of The Grand Stewards' Lodge wears a collar similar to that of a present Grand Steward, though with a Past Grand Steward's jewel suspended from it (Rule 261). Moreover, by long-standing custom, the trimmings of the aprons and collars of present and past Grand Stewards nominated by the Lodge of Antiquity, No. 2, or by British Lodge, No. 8, are gold rather than silver; this is not directly authorised by the Book of Constitutions, but is an extension of Rule 250, which permits the jewels of the Officers of those two Lodges alone to be of gold or metal gilt, rather than of silver.

Of the nineteen red apron Lodges, which annually nominate a Grand Steward for appointment by the Grand Master, some expect those Grand Officers who are Past Grand Stewards (but *not* those who are present or past Provincial or District Grand Stewards) to wear their red regalia to their meetings; others expect those who are Grand Officers to wear their dark blue. There is no general policy in the matter (nor could there be any formal rule in relation to a matter which represents a departure from the Rules in the Book of Constitutions); a Brother who is a Grand Officer as well as a Past Grand Steward will therefore be well advised, if attending as a visitor, to ascertain from his host or the Secretary of the red apron Lodge concerned the policy observed in that particular Lodge.

The Grand Stewards' Lodge, which meets five times a year, holds four of its meetings on the days of the Quarterly Communications of the Grand Lodge – about an hour before the Quarterly Communication begins. Many of its members who are Grand Officers in their own right do not change out of their red regalia into their dark blue, but wear red so as to take advantage of the seats which are reserved, at least in theory, for those Past Grand Stewards who are not Past Grand Officers, under Rule 37.[5]

Gloves and gauntlets

In the Grand Lodge white gloves are an essential part of a Brother's regalia, and they are regarded as such in the majority of Private Lodges. But gloves do not have to be worn in Private Lodges, and many of them did not resume the wearing of gloves after the end of the Second World War, so that there is no overall uniformity. Gloves should be of plain white, and the increasingly common wearing of a pair with a square and compasses design embroidered in blue (or even in white) on the back, at the wrist, is to be deprecated, especially as the angle of the square is frequently less than 90°, thereby making a nonsense of the emblem.

At least in theory, it is within the discretion of the Master of a Lodge whether gloves are to be worn, though it would be a brave Master who went against the established custom in his Lodge, except, perhaps, to dispense with their wearing

---

5   For very many years the seats reserved have been those in the front three rows to the west of the Junior Grand Warden on the south side and the corresponding three rows on the north side of the Grand Temple, rather than "the front bench on each side in the body of the hall" which the Rule continues to prescribe.

in unusually warm weather. If gloves are worn, they should be worn by *all* the Brethren present (including, if they wish, Entered Apprentices and Fellow Crafts) throughout the meeting, except by candidates during the ceremonies of the three degrees and by the Master Elect when actually taking his obligations on the Volume of the Sacred Law.

Gauntlets, which have been briefly mentioned above, were originally long-sleeved gloves worn from medieval times by knights, workmen and others who had a need to protect their wrists and forearms as well as their hands. In a Masonic context such long-sleeved gloves have long since ceased to exist and are nowadays represented by the simple white glove and what amounts to a separate extension of it in the form of a tapering tube of stiffened material (the Book of Constitutions specifies silk) worn over the cuff (so that gauntlets are sometimes called "cuffs"), the whole being contrived to resemble the original one-piece gauntlet; it is therefore a solecism for gauntlets to be worn by the Officers of a Lodge which has dispensed with the wearing of gloves.

Gauntlets are nowadays rarely worn by anyone except the Masters and Wardens of Private Lodges, though they may be worn by all the Officers. In a Private Lodge they are of light blue silk embroidered in silver with the emblem of office within a double circle which generally bears the name and number of the Lodge. Gauntlets may, however, be worn as part of the dress regalia of Grand Officers, Provincial or District Grand Officers, and holders of Metropolitan or Overseas Grand Ranks. In such a case they are of garter-blue with gold embroidery – for Grand Officers the emblem of rank is within a wreath of a sprig of acacia and an ear of corn; for the others it is within a double circle bearing the name of the Province etc. Present or Past Provincial or District Grand Stewards may wear similar gauntlets of crimson with silver embroidery. Grand Stewards and Past Grand Stewards alone are not entitled to wear gauntlets! Because of the elaborate embroidery, gauntlets were an expensive item of regalia and ceased to be a mandatory part of a Grand Officer's dress regalia in 1971, after the Board of General Purposes had examined the historical background to their wearing and concluded "that their use as separate items of regalia is derived rather from change in fashion and as a matter of convenience, than from any real symbolic significance". They have long since ceased to be worn in the Grand Lodge by the Grand Officers of the year. At the time of writing, the only Province where dark blue gauntlets are to be met with as a matter of course is West Lancashire; virtually everywhere else their use has been abandoned.

Visitors and joining members from other Constitutions

A visitor from a recognised Constitution wears his appropriate regalia under the Grand Lodge from which he comes, though if he has set out on his travels without taking the precaution of packing his regalia he may legitimately be lent an English Master Mason's or Installed Master's apron to wear instead. The standard regalia of senior Brethren from other Constitutions may in many cases be the equivalent of English full dress regalia and therefore include a chain. This *they* may wear with perfect propriety in an English Lodge, whatever the Rules in the Book of Constitutions may require for Brethren of the English Constitution.

A Brother, however, from a recognised Constitution who becomes a joining member of an English Lodge is bound by all the provisions of the Book of Constitutions – a copy of which must be presented to him on his election: Rule 163(h) – those on regalia not being excepted. He may therefore no longer wear any of his foreign regalia, including jewels. He *must* wear an English Master Mason's apron, unless he is an Installed Master, in which case he is entitled to "levels" instead of rosettes, but however senior he may be in his Mother Grand Lodge, he may only wear light blue, unless and until he receives a higher rank under this Constitution; nor, until he has served a full year in the Chair of an English Lodge, may he wear a Past Master's collar. It will therefore be seen that, like a Worshipful Master who resigns from his Lodge during his year in office, such a Brother is likely to be a trap for the unsuspecting Director of Ceremonies. As an exception, such a Brother may wear his foreign regalia in the rare instance of his being in attendance on, or representing, his Grand Master on a formal visit (see *Information for the Guidance of Members of the Craft* under the heading "Wearing of Regalia in English Lodges"), but as a matter of established protocol, it is appropriate for another Grand Master to make a formal visit or to request a Brother to represent him *only* in response to a formal invitation extended to him via the respective Grand Secretaries (or, abroad, via the respective District authorities).

Jewels

It would be easy enough to fill an entire chapter on the subject of jewels, but a brief survey must suffice. It cannot be stressed too much that *no jewel* may be worn in the Grand Lodge, a Metropolitan, Provincial or District Grand Lodge or a Private Lodge, "unless it appertains to, or is consistent with, those degrees which are recognised… as part of pure Antient Masonry, and has been approved or allowed by the Grand Master" (Rule 241 – which also covers medals, devices and emblems). Apart from those jewels, already largely dealt with above, which are worn appended to a collar to show the office or rank of the wearer, jewels are usually worn (like medals) on the left breast, but sometimes appended to a collarette. Perhaps because of their relative rarity, the latter (or perhaps the collarettes from which they are suspended) are much more sought after or aspired to than the former. When a collarette is worn, the ribbon should pass *under* the points of the shirt collar, with the inner edge of the collarette hanging about an inch below the knot of the tie. Correspondingly, a breast jewel is what its name implies: it should always be worn on the left breast of the coat or jacket, and *never* on a Brother's Past Master's or other collar.

While there is no actual impropriety in a Brother wearing any Craft or Royal Arch Jewel that satisfies the test in Rule 241, the modern trend is very much towards wearing fewer and fewer breast jewels. Portraits and photographs of Grand Officers in the nineteenth and early twentieth centuries often show them liberally bespangled with jewels, apparently pinned at random on the left breast.[6] For a good many years, however, it has been the practice, if not an actual convention, for Grand Officers to wear no breast jewels other than the Royal Arch Jewel of the Order (*not* a Royal Arch Past First Principal's jewel – see below). Often, however, at the desire of the Provincial Grand Master, during the run-up to a Charity Festival, Grand Officers in a Province will wear the Festival jewel as a means of promoting the Festival, and in London the Founder's Jewel for the Metropolitan Grand Lodge is also commonly worn by Grand Officers.[7] In recent years the practice of wearing none but the Royal Arch jewel has been spreading to Provincial Grand Officers and holders of London Ranks, and it has much to commend it, as the recycling of Past Masters' jewels which it accelerates (a) saves the expense of buying a jewel for each succeeding Past Master and (b) enables the jewels of respected Past Masters to have a prolonged life of usefulness.

---

6   As a matter of convenience Brethren who made a habit of wearing a large number of jewels commonly affixed them more or less permanently on to a strip of black material, which could then be attached in a single operation to the left breast of the coat or jacket. The practice continued well into the middle of the twentieth century.

7   These are examples or illustrations of the point made in the Preface that etiquette and notions of what constitutes "good form" are sometimes dependent on the context and on what other people are doing.

Absolutely taboo are the jewels of other Masonic Orders.[8] Even the Craft jewels of other Masonic Constitutions may not normally be worn, though an exception is made in the case of the dwindling band of senior Grand Officers who have been appointed as Representatives at the United Grand Lodge of England of recognised Grand Lodges and received a jewel to mark their capacity.[9] On those occasions when they visit Lodges under that Constitution, that jewel not only may, but as a matter of etiquette should, be worn, as it should also in an English Lodge if the Grand Master of the Grand Lodge whom they represent is present, or if for some reason they are specially invited to attend in a representative capacity on behalf of that Grand Lodge. Brethren of a less exalted status may, if they have been awarded some *significant* distinction under another Grand Lodge, apply to the Grand Master for a limited permission (which is granted only in an appropriate case) to wear the jewel with their English regalia on much the same occasions as a Representative would wear his jewel.

Jewels fall essentially into two categories: those worn to denote status in the Craft (or Royal Arch) as a whole, and those worn only by the members of a particular Lodge.

Foremost among those in the first category is the Royal Arch Jewel, prescribed by Royal Arch Regulation 85 to be worn by every Royal Arch Companion as part of his Royal Arch regalia (not to be confused with the breast jewel of a Past First Principal of a Chapter, which is far too commonly seen worn with Craft regalia – see below). Its wearing in the Craft is not mandatory, but is very strongly encouraged indeed. Closely related to it are the jewels of the First, Second and Third Grand Principals, Metropolitan Grand Superintendents and Grand Superintendents in and over Provinces or Districts. These may be worn with Craft regalia, usually in slightly miniaturised form, suspended from a collarette of dark

---

8   From time to time, also, it is suggested that during the month of November, or the first part of it, Brethren who have them should be permitted to wear decorations and medals with their Masonic regalia. The view has been taken that is inappropriate for orders, decorations or medals to be worn with Masonic regalia at any time of the year. Life would be the poorer and duller if such things did not exist or were never worn, but they all have their particular place, and just as Masonic jewels would be out of place at a Remembrance Day parade, so medals are out of place in a Masonic meeting. When we enter the Lodge Room we leave our distinctions of ordinary life behind us and are all Brethren.

9   No appointments have been made of Representative of other Grand Lodges since 2002, though the Grand Master continues to appoint Brethren as Representatives of the United Grand Lodge of England near other Grand Lodges.

blue, crimson and light blue and, if worn, take the place of the Royal Arch breast Jewel. These are the only Royal Arch Jewels that may be worn from a collarette with Craft regalia.[10] While Chapter Centenary Jewels, Founder's Jewels, Past First Principals' and any other special Royal Arch Jewels *may* be worn in the Craft, it is better that their wearing is confined to Royal Arch Chapters. Certainly it is wrong in principle to wear a Past First Principal's jewel in substitution for the Royal Arch Jewel itself (rather like wearing an apron without a pair of trousers), and even to wear it in the Craft as well as the Royal Arch Jewel is "not very good form". By the same token, it is "even worse form" for Craft jewels to be worn in Chapters, though in a Province undertaking a Festival for one of the Masonic Charities the wearing of the Stewards' jewel (see below) is often positively encouraged. [11]

Charity Jewels form a sub-category by themselves. They are most commonly met with in the form of those issued by the four principal Masonic Charities in connection with their annual Festivals. Such jewels used to be issued only a short time before a Festival actually took place, so that they could be worn at the Festival by those Brethren serving as Stewards; their wearing was confined to the year in respect of which the Festival concerned was held, unless the Grand Master had given his special approval for a particular jewel to be worn permanently. For the last fifteen years or so, however, approval for the striking of a jewel has commonly been granted five years or more before the Festival is due to be held, so that the jewel can be used as a "marketing-tool" in raising funds for the Charity concerned. Once approval for such a jewel has been given, it may be worn by any Brother (not merely one in the Province undertaking the Festival) who has subscribed the amount necessary to qualify as a Steward for the Festival, and "the year in respect of which the Festival concerned was held" is now interpreted as being the period until the next annual Festival of that Charity. Thereafter it may not be worn, unless it has been made a permanent jewel.[12]

---

10 Although within their respective Metropolitan Areas, Provinces and Districts (but only in the particular Metropolitan Area, Province or District) a Past Deputy Grand Superintendent or a Past Second or Third Metropolitan, Provincial or District Grand Principal (and, in London, also a Past Assistant Metropolitan Grand Superintendent) may wear the jewel showing his past rank suspended from a collarette with Royal Arch regalia, such a collarette and jewel must not be worn by him with Craft regalia.

11 This is another illustration of the point, referred to earlier, made in the Preface.

12 As a matter of practice, a successful Festival is customarily marked by the jewel being made a permanent jewel for the Brethren of the host Province.

There is also a Grand Lodge Charity Jewel, which is described in all its many and increasingly elaborate variations in Rule 253 of the Book of Constitutions. To qualify to wear it, a Brother must have served as Steward for a Festival of at least two of the following Charities, namely the Royal Masonic Institution for Girls, the Royal Masonic Institution for Boys and the Royal Masonic Benevolent Institution. As the first two of those Charities ceased to exist nearly thirty years ago on being combined into the Masonic Trust for Girls and Boys (now the *Royal Masonic Trust for Girls and Boys*), it will be seen that the number of those entitled to wear the Charity Jewel is steadily diminishing and that in time the jewel will "wither on the vine". It is still, however, to be met with today, though usually only in one of the more elaborate variations worn by qualified Brethren from a collarette – and it used to be said, perhaps unkindly, that such Brethren wore their charity receipts around their necks.

The Hall Stone Jewel (known until 1964 as the Hall Stone Medal, and so inscribed on the reverse) is of silver gilt worn suspended from a light blue collarette by the Master of a Lodge which subscribed an average of ten guineas per head towards the Masonic Million Memorial Fund, which was set up in 1919 to finance the building of the present Freemasons' Hall as a Peace Memorial. It may (and should) be worn by the Master of a Hall Stone Lodge on all occasions when Craft regalia is worn. Being an item of regalia (see Rule 251, Book of Constitutions, and *Information for the Guidance of Members of the Craft*), it should not be worn by the Master at the dinner (or in the bar before dinner) if there are non-Masons present as waiters or bar staff, unless a dispensation has been given for the wearing of regalia at the after-proceedings. A permanent dispensation exists within the Province of Buckinghamshire – the only Hall Stone Province – for the wearing of the jewel by the Masters of Buckinghamshire Lodges (but only within the Province). The Provincial Grand Master for Buckinghamshire wears a larger Hall Stone Jewel of gold, enamelled in its proper colours, to mark the achievement of his Province. One occasionally sees a Hall Stone Jewel which has been refurbished by the replacement of the collarette from which it is worn with a new (and clean) one of an incorrect "v" shape. The correct pattern is the simplest one possible: a light blue ribbon with a hook at one end and an eye at the other, to fasten it round the wearer's neck, which is threaded through the elongated loop on the top of the jewel, as clearly illustrated in Plate 58 of the Appendix to the Rules in the Book of Constitutions.

The 275th Anniversary breast jewel issued in 1992 may still be worn by those who were members of an English Constitution Lodge at the time of the

Anniversary and who subscribed for it. Similar considerations apply from time to time when a permanent commemorative jewel is authorised for the whole Craft (or for a particular part of it, as with the Founder's Jewels for the Metropolitan Grand Lodge and Metropolitan Grand Chapter of London).

A Grand Officer who is a Past Deputy or Assistant Metropolitan, Provincial or District Grand Master may wear the jewel of a past holder of that office suspended from a "v"-shaped garter-blue collarette, one and a quarter inches wide edged with gold cord. This collarette and jewel may be worn in *any* Lodge and not just those of the Metropolitan Area, Province or District concerned.

The Prestonian Lecturer of the year wears a special jewel, and Past Prestonian Lecturers wear a slightly different version of the same jewel, in each case appended to a dark blue collarette (of the simple ribbon variety, like that for the Hall Stone Jewel).

Finally, and in the place of honour among those jewels which relate to the whole Craft, is the Jewel of a holder of the Grand Master's Order of Service to Masonry. This is of the pattern illustrated in Plate 24 of the Appendix to the Rules in the Book of Constitutions, and is suspended from a dark blue collarette of the simple ribbon variety. The Order is limited to twelve holders at any one time, and it has not been often in recent times that all twelve places have been filled. When it was introduced in 1946, it carried with it precedence as the lowest of the categories of Very Worshipful Brethren, but it was removed from the order of precedence in 1961, so that it could be awarded to any Brother, however junior. Although the Order no longer carries any precedence, the letters "OSM" nonetheless precede all other Masonic designations after the name of one of its holders. Until London Rank (on the new scheme) was introduced in 1998, it was the only honour or promotion that could be conferred on a Master Mason who belonged only to a Lodge in London.

The jewels specific to particular Lodges need not detain us long. Commonest among these are Past Masters' Jewels, generally worn on the breast but occasionally from a collarette; the designs of these often (and in former days almost invariably did) incorporate a device peculiar to the individual Lodge – generally the same device as for the Founders' Jewels (see below) – and are therefore subject to the approval of the Grand Master under Rule 241. A Past Master's Jewel may be worn by or presented to a Brother only after his successor has been installed in the Chair of the Lodge, so that a Master who serves for two years in succession only becomes entitled to such a jewel at the end of the second year. A Brother who serves for a second term after a break may have the fact recorded by a bar on the ribbon. As an elementary courtesy to the Lodge which has presented him with a Past Master's Jewel, a Brother who has not reached a rank where he wears only the Royal Arch Jewel should always wear his Past Master's Jewel in that Lodge.

A Lodge which can establish that it has worked regularly without interruption for one hundred years is entitled to a Centenary Warrant authorising its members of the rank of Master Mason and above to wear the Centenary Jewel illustrated in Plate 59 of the Appendix, and one that can prove two hundred years' uninterrupted working is entitled to a Bi-Centenary bar on the ribbon of the Centenary Jewel. The jewel may be worn by the *subscribing* members of the Lodge, irrespective of whether they were members at the time of the Centenary (or Bi-Centenary), and by former subscribing members who have been elected to Honorary Membership within a year of ceasing to be subscribing members.

Founders' Jewels have already been mentioned. A small replica of the jewel of the office originally held may be worn on the ribbon of the jewel. Many such jewels are so designed that if the Brother concerned subsequently goes through the Chair of the Lodge his Founder's Jewel can be converted to a Past Master's Jewel by the addition of the Past Master's emblem pendent from the ribbon.

A small number of Lodges have a special Member's Jewel for which authority has been given by the Grand Master.

Masonic mourning

A final word will be in order on the subject of Masonic mourning. In its full form, this used (and may still do in some places) to consist of three black rosettes worn on the bottom corners and the point of the flap of the apron (not obscuring the rosettes of a Master Mason or the "levels" of an Installed Master) and, where a collar is worn, a further black rosette worn at the point of the collar covering the junction with the jewel. In Freemasonry, however, as in most other areas of life, mourning is far less ostentatiously observed nowadays than was formerly the case. The rosettes on the apron are hardly ever met with, and even a rosette on the point of the collar has become uncommon. When the late Bro. The Earl Cadogan, Past Pro Grand Master, died in 1997, the form of mourning then ordered was a single rosette on the collars or chains of present Grand Officers, present Provincial or District Grand Officers and the Masters, Wardens and other Officers of Private Lodges. The period of mourning was limited to three months, instead of the six months which had previously been common. When the late Bro. Lord Farnham, Past Pro Grand Master, died in 2001, mourning was not ordered to be worn, and it therefore seems unlikely that mourning will be ordered for the Craft as a whole in future. In a Metropolitan Area, Province or District the matter lies within the discretion of the Metropolitan, Provincial or District Grand Master, who may therefore take his own view having regard to local tradition, and conditions at the time.

3

MEMBERSHIP

A LODGE is a place where free-masons assemble to work and to instruct and improve themselves in the mysteries of the antient science. In an extended sense it applies to persons as well as to place; hence every regular assembly or duly organised meeting of masons is called a lodge. Every brother ought to belong to some lodge, and be subject to its by-laws and the general regulations of the craft. A lodge may be either general or particular, as will be best understood by attending it, and there a knowledge of the established usages and customs of the craft is alone to be acquired. From antient times no master or fellow could be absent from his lodge, especially when warned to appear at it, without incurring a severe censure, unless it appeared to the master and wardens that pure necessity hindered him.

The persons made masons or admitted members of a lodge must be good and true men, free-born, and of mature and discreet age and sound judgement, no bondmen, no women, no immoral or scandalous men, but of good report.

THE CHARGES OF A FREE-MASON – III Of LODGES

Every Freemason starts his Masonic career as an initiate and – except for that increasingly rare individual, the Serving Brother – as a subscribing member of a Lodge (see Rule 166 of the Book of Constitutions). For many, that is the only category of membership that they will ever fall within, but there are four distinct categories into which Freemasons may fall, and various ways of acquiring membership of a Lodge.

Subscribing Members
Subscribing members are by far the most common. Until the 1970s, when the cost of dining suddenly increased dramatically, subscribing members were usually

divided into two categories: full members, who paid a subscription that included the cost of all the Lodge dinners during the course of the year, and those who paid a reduced subscription because – in the words of Rule 145 of the Book of Constitutions – they were "for some cause satisfactory to the Lodge, ... not in a position to enjoy such privileges regularly". The latter, on those occasions when they chose – or were able – to dine, paid a dining fee (usually that charged for guests of the members). Economic and social factors have made full dining membership much less common than it once was, so that today "full" members enjoy for their subscription merely all the privileges that the particular Lodge offers to its members, often no longer automatically including the Lodge dinners (but sometimes allowing "full" members to dine at a reduced dining fee). The second category, if it exists in the particular Lodge, may be called "country", "overseas" or "non-dining" members, depending on the nature of the privileges enjoyed by the full members.

Honorary Members

A Lodge may also have Honorary Members, elected under Rule 167 after notice on the summons. Note that unlike candidates for initiation and joining, these do not have to have been proposed and seconded at the meeting before they are balloted for, and *three* black balls are necessary to prevent their election. An Honorary Member may be "any Brother of good standing and worthy of such distinction by reason of his services to the Craft, or to the particular Lodge, who is, or within the previous year has been, a subscribing member of a regular Lodge". He will therefore usually have been a distinguished subscribing member of the Lodge, elected (often when his financial or other circumstances have caused him to resign) in recognition of his services to it or to the Craft, but he may be a non-member elected to mark either a general contribution to the Craft or a special contribution to the Lodge. For example, it is the almost universal practice to elect as Honorary Members the Consecrating Officers of a new Lodge, or, though more rarely, the members of an official deputation attending a special meeting of the Lodge to mark its Centenary or other notable anniversary. Some Lodges make it their usual practice to elect their Provincial Grand Master; others pride themselves on having had, for example, every Grand Secretary for the last so-many years as an Honorary Member. In these days when fewer and fewer Brethren are capable of playing the piano, let alone an organ, it is becoming common to elect to Honorary Membership a Brother who, over the years (sometimes not very many years), has as a visitor played the organ for a Lodge's ceremonies.

A Brother elected an Honorary Member does not have to be a member of a Lodge under this Constitution; in certain Lodges with a special connection with another country it is not unusual to elect to Honorary Membership the Grand Master, and sometimes other senior Brethren, of the Grand Lodge associated with that country.

It should never be forgotten that Honorary Membership is a privilege. No one has a right to demand it or to feel aggrieved if he does not receive it. Some Provincial Grand Masters in the not too distant past have let it be known by one means or other that they expected to be elected Honorary Members of all the Lodges in their Province – and thereby betrayed their lack of understanding of the nature of Honorary Membership. I myself remember in another Order a former secretary who, having resigned through age and ill health, kept writing to complain that he had not been made an Honorary Member.

Honorary Membership carries with it certain disabilities, actual or potential. Lodges should therefore be aware before electing a subscribing member to Honorary Membership (and should make sure that he too is aware) that if he will then no longer be a subscribing member of any Lodge he will become an unattached Mason (see below). Moreover, he may not hold any office in the Lodge [1] (other than that of Tyler – Rule 104(b)) and cannot vote on any matter, though a former subscribing member, if a Past Master, may propose and second candidates.

Honorary Membership has its own etiquette – on both sides – but to complicate matters it varies considerably from Lodge to Lodge. At the most basic level, an Honorary Member has the undoubted right to attend every meeting of the Lodge as well as to receive summonses and, if they are circulated, minutes. Not every Lodge is as diligent in this matter of summonses and minutes as it ought to be, but an Honorary Member is still a member of the Lodge – and if the Lodge cared enough about him to elect him an Honorary Member it should show that it still cares by maintaining regular contact in this rather rudimentary way.

Beyond this, if there is one overriding rule it is that there are no hard and fast rules, and the extent to which an Honorary Member should exercise his privileges is a matter in which considerable tact may be called for. Perhaps the question that most exercises an Honorary Member is whether he should pay for his meal. Some Lodges make a point of specially inviting their Honorary Members to certain meetings, and it is then not hard to divine that the Lodge intends them on such occasions to be their guests (but probably not on others). Clearly, however, no

---

1   He may, of course, carry out the duties of any Officer as a stand-in, either in the absence of the regular holder of the office, or if specially requested to do so.

Honorary Member can expect to enjoy greater privileges than a full subscribing member, so that if the normal Lodge subscription does not include the meal, an Honorary Member should certainly expect to pay. Even when the Lodge has a full dining subscription, an Honorary Member should exercise discretion; one who attends perhaps one meeting every two or three years will be more welcome than one who elects to attend every other meeting, and if the latter wishes to retain his place in the hearts and affections of the members he will do well to *insist* on paying his way. There will be obvious exceptions, such as the guest Organist for whom the Lodge will expect, and indeed intend, to pay the cost of his meal.

Another question that sometimes arises is whether an Honorary Member may properly invite a guest to the Lodge. The better view is that as there is nothing in the Book of Constitutions to forbid it, unless the Lodge's by-laws expressly preclude it, he may do so – but clearly it must be at his own expense. Here, though, as in other areas, tact is called for and an Honorary Member should avoid abusing his privileges by using them to excess.

An Honorary Member should not forget that he has no vote in the affairs of the Lodge and should be as cautious about volunteering advice as he would be if he were a visitor. Finally, Honorary Membership can be terminated in the same way as subscribing membership, so that an Honorary Member can resign as such and can also be excluded under Rule 181 – though not, as he pays no subscription, under Rule 148.

Unattached Brethren

A Freemason who has ceased, for whatever reason, to be a subscribing member of all his Lodges is described as "unattached" and must write that word after his name in the attendance book of a Lodge, together with the name and number of the Lodge of which he was last a subscribing member, when exercising his strictly limited right to visit. His position is governed by Rule 127 of the Book of Constitutions, which also indirectly imposes a serious disability on a Brother who is elected to Honorary Membership if he does not retain at least one subscribing membership. The Rule precludes a Brother who becomes unattached by resignation while in good standing with his Lodge, or by election as an Honorary Member, [2] from visiting any single Lodge *more than once for all time* (not, as is

---

2   An Honorary Member, even though unattached, has an unrestricted right to attend any
    Lodge of which he is an Honorary Member (Rule 127).

often supposed, once a year), though he has an unrestricted right to attend Lodges of Instruction; and if he is a Grand Officer he retains his membership of, and the right to attend, the Grand Lodge (but not of any Metropolitan, Provincial or District Grand Lodge) under Rule 2. The plight of a Brother who becomes unattached as a result of his exclusion under Rule 148 or 181 is still less attractive, as he is precluded from visiting *any* Lodge or Lodge of Instruction until he again becomes a subscribing member of a Lodge. Moreover, if not a Grand Officer, he can only regain his right to attend Grand Lodge as a Past Master by serving once more as Master of a Lodge (Rule 9).

Serving Brethren

The final category of member is that of Serving Brother. This status is an interesting historical survival and almost, but not quite, a dead letter. In the eighteenth century when much of a Lodge's work was carried on at table, with the Lodge being called on and off as the occasion demanded, it was necessary to ensure that, besides the meeting, the meal also, if possible, was tyled throughout. This meant that it was desirable that, besides the Tyler, the waiters also should be Freemasons so that they could discreetly carry out their duties without interrupting the Lodge. The initiation fee in those days of a guinea or more, as well as the subscription to a Lodge, was far beyond the means of those employed as Tylers or as waiters in the inns and taverns where Lodges met, and so it became the practice to make them Serving Brethren without the need of paying a fee, serving the Lodge which initiated them and others meeting at the same premises.

Rule 170 of the Book of Constitutions regulates the position today, though the economic conditions that led to the creation of the status no longer apply throughout most of the world. Today, a Serving Brother may only be initiated by dispensation, and though neither initiation fee nor registration fee has to be paid, he must himself pay for his Grand Lodge Certificate (at a reduced fee), which is in the normal form, but specially enfaced with a statement that he was initiated as a Serving Brother. [3] He enjoys (if that is the appropriate word) a peculiarly hobbled status: he is a regular Mason and may serve "his" Lodge and others as Tyler (a Tyler must be registered in the books of Grand Lodge as a Master Mason, but he does not have to be a subscribing member of a Lodge), but his position is

---

3   "Issued to the within named Brother as a Serving Brother pursuant to Rule 170, Book of Constitutions."

even less enviable than that of an unattached Mason, as he may not visit *any* Lodge. An escape route is provided for him in the Rule which allows him to become a joining member of a Lodge (not necessarily that which initiated him) for which he must pay the *initiation* fee then current, and from that moment he enjoys all the rights and privileges he would have had if he had not been initiated as a Serving Brother. The normal registration fee must be paid and he is then entitled to exchange his Serving Brother's Certificate free of charge for a normal Grand Lodge Certificate bearing the same date as the original.

If I have dealt at greater length with Serving Brethren than might seem justified in view of their rarity, it is because the status of Serving Brother is so often misunderstood. Far too commonly one hears a Tyler referred to as a Serving Brother – but he hardly ever is. I have even seen a request from a holder of London Grand Rank to be permitted to change his status to that of a Serving Brother, completely failing to understand that any movement could only be in the opposite direction. What he actually wanted to do was relinquish his subscribing membership of his Lodge and confine his Masonic activity to tyling. This points out a useful lesson: do not rush to use an expression you have seen somewhere or heard someone else use unless you are *sure* that you know what it means. If in doubt, look it up!

Registration Forms, the Lewis and Initiation

Except for the Founders of a new Lodge, who subscribe their names to a Petition, and Honorary Members, who are not required to complete any paperwork, the first step in becoming a member of a Lodge is the completion of a Registration Form. The form has, for good reason, become increasingly complex over the years and now runs to four A4 pages with sections to be completed by the candidate, his proposer and seconder, the Master, the Secretary and, in certain cases, the Grand Secretary. A candidate for initiation has to subscribe to a declaration that he has not, among other things, been the subject of criminal or similar proceedings, and the same is required of an unattached Mason who seeks to join or rejoin a Lodge after a period of Masonic inactivity. If an unqualified declaration cannot be made, the form has to be sent, with a statement of the circumstances that prevent a clean declaration from being made, to the Grand Secretary for a certificate that the matters disclosed do not (if such be the case) constitute a bar to initiation or resuming a Masonic career, as the case may be – Rule 164(a)(ii). While the certificate of the Grand Secretary has to be read out in Lodge at the time the candidate is proposed and again before the ballot is taken, the *details* of the candidate's "shady past" do not have to be. When the declaration was introduced, some Brethren regarded it as intrusive ("I shall never introduce one of my friends as a candidate if I have to insult him by asking him about such things") but, as has just been shown, the procedure has been quite sensitively structured and has now achieved general acceptance.

The status and privileges of a Lewis are often misunderstood. A Lewis is the uninitiated son of a Mason, so that the statement from a Brother that he *is* a Lewis, rather than that he *was* a Lewis is misconceived. It is sometimes asserted that a Lewis has a right to be initiated at eighteen, instead of at the usual age of twenty-one, or, where a Lodge has (unusually these days) a waiting list of candidates, that he is entitled to go to the head of the queue, but neither statement is true. The sole privilege of a Lewis is, when more than one candidate is initiated on the same day, to be the first of them. (See *Information for the Guidance of Members of the Craft.*)

The question often arises of how long a proposer and seconder must have known a candidate in order to sponsor him. There is no easy answer to this question. The Book of Constitutions gives no help here, beyond the requirement in Rule 159 that, "The proposer and seconder of a candidate must either be subscribing members of the Lodge, or be qualified in this respect by Rule 167; the candidate must be personally known to them and they must be able to state that he is a man of good reputation and well fitted to become a member of the Lodge." Depth of knowledge is at least as important as length of acquaintance, and it is easily possible to know a man's character far better after a few weeks in close proximity to him than after ten or more years of mere passing familiarity. The Registration Form has for some twenty years contained a series of questions designed to elicit the depth of the sponsors' familiarity with their candidate, which provides useful guidance to the Lodge Committee when it interviews the latter.

In these days, when Provinces and even Lodges periodically hold open days to increase public awareness and understanding of Freemasonry, and almost every Province has its own website, it is by no means uncommon for Provinces or individual Lodges to receive an approach from a potential candidate who is unknown to them – or to any Freemason in the locality. Provincial authorities have generally evolved their own strategies for dealing with this situation, and Lodges should therefore seek guidance from them. It is undoubtedly sensible, however short of candidates a Lodge may be, to avoid rushing to take anyone as a candidate until some at least of the members have got to know him and have satisfied themselves that he is right for Freemasonry (and Freemasonry right for him) and that he will fit into the particular Lodge. Many individuals may be exactly right for Freemasonry but not right for the Lodge they have managed to get themselves initiated in, and few things will kill a new Brother's enthusiasm for the Craft more surely than finding that he is in a Lodge whose place, dates or times of meeting are inconvenient, or with whose members he finds he has little in common. A Lodge may find that it is able to short-circuit a little the process of getting to know a candidate if he proves to be known to other Freemasons, perhaps geographically remote but able to vouch for his suitability. One of the best candidates one of my Lodges has taken within the last few years knew no one in the Lodge but was a good friend of a Provincial Grand Officer in a Province about 100 miles away. I was able to speak to the latter's Provincial Grand Secretary, who confirmed that he would gladly back his fellow Provincial Grand Officer's judgement, and, being that year the Master, I had the pleasure of initiating him.

Relatively new Masons would be wise not to rush too quickly to introduce their friends into their Lodge; they may themselves not yet have acquired settled views on the Craft and therefore not yet be able to reach a balanced assessment of their friends' suitability for Freemasonry (and vice versa). Also, other longer-established members (not necessarily by any means the most senior) may feel uncomfortable with a new member introducing candidates in any quantity. (Indeed, it can be a "danger signal" in any Lodge if a very small number of Brethren introduce most or many of its candidates.) Conversely, I have known senior Past Masters tell a Brother that he is far too junior in the Lodge to introduce a candidate, or – only slightly better – that his candidate is perfectly suitable, but that he is too junior to propose him, and that therefore one of the Past Masters will do it instead. The latter attitude can be entirely well intentioned, to avoid saddling a young member with responsibility if his candidate later proves to have been a mistake, but even if that is the reason it can be seen as patronising, and as a matter of *principle* there is no reason why an Entered Apprentice or a Fellow Craft, provided that the Lodge Committee is satisfied with the candidate, should not be his proposer or seconder.

Rule 157 of the Book of Constitutions provides that no person may be made a Mason under the age of twenty-one except by dispensation. No minimum age is provided in the Rule, but it is generally considered to be eighteen. Previously there was an understanding that such dispensations would be granted only for undergraduate members of the Universities of Oxford and Cambridge to enable them to be initiated in Apollo University Lodge, No. 357 or Isaac Newton

University Lodge, No. 859 respectively. Since 2001, however, every case for a dispensation has been considered on its merits, the test being whether the candidate is of mature age and sound judgement (as well as a free man and in reputable circumstances).

If a candidate seeks initiation in a Lodge in a *locality* where he has neither a permanent place of residence nor a regular place of business or employment, then the provisions of Rule 158 must be followed. This Rule is one of the most frequently misunderstood in the Book of Constitutions, so much so that in June 1989 the Board of General Purposes devoted a substantial part of its Report to the scope, purpose and application of the Rule. The relevant paragraphs from the Report are reprinted annually in the booklet *Information for the Guidance of Members of the Craft*. The purpose of the Rule is to prevent individuals whose local reputation is such that they cannot gain admission to a Lodge near the place where they live or work from seeking initiation at some distant place where they are unknown, and the significant word here is "locality". A candidate living at one end of even a small Province who seeks initiation in a Lodge at the other end of it should almost certainly be the subject of an enquiry under the Rule, while a candidate living in another Province, but only a mile or two distant from the place where the Lodge meets should equally certainly not be.

An enquiry under the Rule should be directed to the relevant Metropolitan, Provincial or District Grand Secretary, and is an enquiry into the local reputation of the candidate. It is therefore not the responsibility of the recipient of the enquiry to arrange for the candidate to be interviewed – that is a matter for the Lodge's own committee – but to find out by whatever means are appropriate (most often by enquiring of the Lodges meeting in the locality) what, if any, reputation the candidate has. It is equally inappropriate for the recipient of the enquiry to treat it as a request for permission to initiate the candidate, so that a reply to the effect that "the Provincial Grand Master has no objection to your Lodge initiating Mr. Blank" is misconceived.

Where the normal procedure of proposing and seconding a candidate for initiation at one meeting and balloting for him at the next, "would impose serious hardship" upon him a "fast track" procedure is available under Rule 160, which provides that a proposer and seconder may in such a case send the Master details of their candidate together with a statement of the reasons for him to be initiated as a matter of urgency. "If in the opinion of the Master the urgency be real, and that hardship upon the candidate would be serious" the candidate may be proposed and balloted for at the same meeting (which may be an emergency meeting) and if elected he *must* thereupon be initiated. The cause of the urgency and the nature of the hardship must be specified in the summons, stated in open Lodge before the ballot is taken, and recorded in the minutes.

It should be noted, first – and most importantly – that this is the *only* situation in which, under the Rules in the Book of Constitutions, a candidate for initiation or joining may be proposed and seconded, or balloted for, at an emergency meeting. Secondly, that there must be hardship, which must be serious, to the *candidate*; hardship to the Lodge or one or more of its members is nothing to the point. Thirdly, that there must be some urgency in the matter, though not necessarily exclusively to the candidate. Finally, that the Master is the arbiter both of the hardship and the urgency, for which the Rule lays down no test and provides no guidance.

The procedure under Rule 160 is intended for exceptional circumstances, and should be treated with the respect it deserves. It should certainly not be used as a let-out for the carelessness of the Secretary or the dilatoriness of a candidate's sponsors. The Master should also be aware that, though he is the arbiter – and for the purposes of the Rule the sole arbiter – of the hardship and the urgency, and though the initiation once it has taken place cannot be undone even if the Rule has been used inappropriately, he is not beyond the reach of higher Masonic authority and could, at least in theory, be disciplined for bringing Freemasonry into disrepute if he allows the Rule to be misused.

Founders, amalgamations and joining members

Under the United Grand Lodge of England, unlike some other Grand Lodges, there is no restriction on the number of Lodges to which a Brother may belong. In fact, however, somewhere between 80 and 85 per cent of English Constitution Masons belong only to a single Lodge, and of the rest about three-quarters belong to two Lodges only. Some will have acquired a second or subsequent membership by being Founders of new Lodges, others by a transfer of membership on an amalgamation, but by far the greatest number are simple joining members.

Before coming to the procedure for joining members, a word or two is in order about new Lodges and amalgamations. To form a new Lodge, at least seven Petitioners are required, all of whom at the date of signing the Petition must be Master Masons of at least three years' standing. If the Lodge is to meet in London or a Province, all the Petitioners must be registered in the books of the United Grand Lodge of England, but if it is to meet abroad not more than three-sevenths of the Petitioners may be duly registered members of another Constitution recognised by the United Grand Lodge of England, provided that they have signed the declaration of obedience prescribed by Rule 163(f) – see below. Every Petitioner must specify on the Petition every Lodge of which he is or has at any time been a member and produce a clearance certificate from each of them. Every Petition must be recommended by an existing Lodge (which need have no connection with the locality where the proposed Lodge is to meet), for which purpose it must, following notice on the summons for the meeting, be approved by a majority of the members *present* and signed by the Master and Wardens *in open Lodge*. The Petition must then be forwarded to the Grand Secretary for the Grand Master's decision, via the relevant Metropolitan, Provincial or District Grand Master, if any, with his observations. It can thus be seen that the process is at least as rigorous as for joining membership and cannot be regarded as a short cut.

On an amalgamation a simplified procedure has been devised to transfer the members of the Amalgamating Lodge or Lodges (as defined in Rule 165A) to the continuing Lodge. A joint (or "block") Registration Form, incorporating a joint clearance certificate to be signed by the Master and Secretary, is completed by the Brethren wishing to transfer their membership. Their names are then placed on the summons for a regular meeting of the continuing Lodge to be held *not later than* the date when the amalgamation will become effective and, provided that two-thirds of the members of the continuing Lodge present and voting vote to accept them (a show of hands is sufficient), their membership is automatically transferred at the moment the amalgamation takes effect (*i.e.* when the Grand Lodge votes to remove the Amalgamating Lodge or Lodges from the Register of the Grand Lodge). The simplified procedure may not be used in the case of a Brother who is in arrears to the Amalgamating Lodge at the time, or who has *at any time* been excluded from *any Lodge* under Rule 148 or Rule 181. This does not mean that such a Brother may not participate in the amalgamation, only that he must go through the normal procedure of joining the continuing Lodge. Moreover, the procedure is not effective to transfer the membership of any Brother who proves to have been, at the date when the amalgamation became effective, indebted to any Lodge of which he was then, or had at any time been, a member. This appears to be the only instance of membership, once fully taken up, subsequently being invalidated, and may give rise to difficulty at some future date – though so far it has not done so.

Rule 163 of the Book of Constitutions specifically relates to joining members, who must in every case be proposed and seconded at one regular meeting and balloted for at the next; there is no short cut to joining membership. A candidate for joining must list every Lodge (under *any* Constitution) of which he is or has at any time been a subscribing member, and before he is balloted for he must produce a "clearance certificate" (see below) from each of them, as well as his Grand Lodge Certificate, to the Secretary. If a Lodge takes a joining member in the knowledge that he has undischarged arrears owing to a Lodge from which he has been excluded or resigned it makes itself liable to that Lodge for those arrears – Rule 163(d).

Just as a candidate for initiation must be initiated within a year of his election or the election is void (Rule 159), so a candidate elected a joining member must, by Rule 163(a), take up his membership within a year. In this context a year means a calendar year of 365 days, not from that meeting until the meeting at the corresponding period in the following year. Here, the question is often asked as to what constitutes taking up membership, perhaps by a Secretary for the purpose of submitting the Annual Return, or by a candidate elected at the very end of a subscription year who wishes to delay the start of his membership to the start of the next subscription year. The Book of Constitutions gives no direct guidance on this question, and so the answer has to be a matter of common sense. If the candidate is present on the occasion of the ballot, his membership clearly takes effect from the moment he is readmitted to the Lodge and presented with the by-laws in accordance with Rule 138. But a candidate is not always present at the meeting at which the ballot is taken; what then? The test, it is suggested, is whether the candidate has committed any act which is consistent only with his having accepted that he is a member of the Lodge. So the payment of his joining fee and subscription to the Treasurer clearly satisfies the test; so does attending a meeting, proposing a candidate or inviting a guest; so, it is suggested, does returning his card before a meeting with a statement that he will not be present.

A Brother joining from another Constitution must, by Rule 163(e), be the subject of an enquiry to the Grand Secretary (or in a District, the District Grand Secretary) to ascertain that the other Constitution is recognised by the United Grand Lodge of England, and he must, on his election or within a year thereafter, make the declaration of obedience prescribed by Rule 163(f). Until the declaration has been made the election is not valid, even though the candidate may have paid his joining fee and subscription, and if it is not made within the year, the election lapses.

Clearance certificates

A Brother is entitled to, and a Lodge is obliged to give him free of charge, a certificate under Rule 175, *whenever he requires it*, stating either that he is a member and that he is or is not indebted to it, or that he was formerly a member, giving the circumstances under which he left it (*i.e.* resignation or exclusion), that he was or was not indebted to it and whether (and, if so, when) any such indebtedness was discharged. A certificate complying with the Rule is generally called a "clearance certificate", even though it may show that a Brother is *not* clear in the books of his Lodge or former Lodge. A Lodge may not under any circumstances refuse a certificate if one is requested, and nothing can justify a refusal – though I have twice known instances where a refusal has occurred. A refusal is a serious matter and should be expected to give rise to disciplinary action against the Lodge or against any of its Officers responsible for it.

There is no prescribed form for a clearance certificate. It is desirable that it should be on the headed paper of the Lodge,[4] and at its most basic it must state, besides the date, that the Brother is a member of the Lodge and (if such be the case) is not indebted to it. A helpful Lodge Secretary, however, will amplify the information at least a little. When a Brother is still a member of the Lodge the "shelf life" of a clearance certificate can never exceed twelve months, and a certificate that contains only the date of issue should never be assumed to be valid beyond the end of that month. An additional statement therefore that the Brother is fully paid up to, say, 31 December immediately renders the certificate more useful.

It is the Brother himself who is entitled to the certificate. In my younger days it was not uncommon for a Lodge Secretary to adopt a rather proprietorial attitude towards a clearance certificate and insist on sending it direct to the Secretary of the Lodge requiring it, or, reversing the situation, to write direct to the other Secretary requesting it. The attitude was mistaken: a clearance certificate is a simple statement of what should be verifiable fact; it is not a testimonial or a confidential reference, and if it contains any adverse report the Brother is entitled to know of it.

When the Brother is no longer a member of the Lodge, if he left it in good financial standing, his clearance certificate will be valid for all time. It is therefore a matter of at least common courtesy and consideration on his part to keep it carefully and avoid parting with it unless it is necessary for him to do so, rather than rely on his unfettered right to require a certificate at any time. If it is some time since his membership ceased, the Secretary or Treasurer may be put to

---

4   It is highly undesirable that a clearance certificate should be given by e-mail. A Brother requesting a certificate and a Lodge Secretary to whom it is provided should insist on a paper certificate bearing an original signature of the Secretary or other Officer of the Lodge issuing it.

considerable trouble in verifying the circumstances in which he left. Lodge records have been known to be mislaid, and Lodges themselves cease to exist, with the result that a certificate has then to be obtained from the Grand Secretary stating the facts so far as they are known – Rule 163(c).

Rule 175 requires that except as provided by the Rule no Lodge shall grant a Certificate of any kind to a Brother. This has sometimes led to overzealous Masonic administrators coming down heavily on Lodges wishing to present a Brother with some form of testimonial – perhaps in the form of an illuminated address or "certificate" – to mark some special event or "milestone" in his Masonic career. While such a document may, because of the way it is worded, fall within the definition of a Certificate, it is not the sort of mischief at which the Rule is aimed, and common sense should be allowed to prevail.

Termination of membership

It is appropriate to end this chapter on membership with a discussion of the ways in which membership, either of the Craft itself or of an individual Lodge, may itself be ended.

Membership of the Craft is most commonly terminated by death, but it can also come to an end by expulsion, enforced resignation following an invitation to resign issued by the Grand Secretary under Rule 277A, or voluntary resignation under Rule 183A of the Book of Constitutions. Expulsion and resignation under Rule 277A are both disciplinary penalties which can be imposed only following disciplinary proceedings by a Masonic authority and, in the case of expulsion, confirmation by an Appeals Court. Voluntary resignation from the Craft may be either for personal reasons or to avoid disciplinary sanctions, and is considered further below.

Resignation from a Lodge

Membership of a particular Lodge is most commonly terminated by resignation from the Lodge under Rule 183. A Brother may resign orally in open Lodge, either with immediate effect or from a later date which he then specifies. He would be well advised, however, not to adopt this method except after careful consideration, because the resignation once spoken is irrevocable unless the Lodge votes immediately that he be invited to withdraw it; in which case he will have twenty-one days in which to reconsider, and if he withdraws it within the time allowed his resignation will be considered cancelled.

The more usual method of resigning is by written notice to the Secretary, again either with immediate effect or from a later specified date. The Secretary is obliged to report the resignation to the Lodge at the next *regular* meeting, unless the Brother has withdrawn it in the meantime, and once communicated to the Lodge it becomes irrevocable (unless the Lodge votes to give him twenty-one days to reconsider) and takes effect from the date the Secretary received it, or from such later date as may have been specified. The opportunity for the Brother to change his mind before the next regular meeting makes this the more sensible method for him to use, unless he is absolutely determined to resign.

Two points need to be noted. First, that whichever method is used, once the resignation is communicated to the Lodge (unless time is given for reconsideration) it becomes irrevocable, *even though expressed to take effect at a later date, however distant.* Secondly, that the written notice must be to the Secretary. It is not uncommon for a Brother, paying late, to send a cheque with his outstanding subscription to the Treasurer together with his resignation. Although the Rule is quite specific as to the procedure, it is a matter of etiquette for the Treasurer to draw the Brother's attention to the requirements of the Rule, even if he only does so in some such form as, "I am passing your resignation to the Secretary, to whom the Rules require it to be given." Enforcement of the strict letter of the Rule without warning him, particularly if the start of the new subscription year is not many days away, would be regarded by many as un-Masonic, and in any case is liable to give rise to recriminations which could have been avoided. A similar observation applies with even greater force if communication is to the Master, Almoner or some other member of the Lodge, or is made orally, perhaps by telephone. The Board of General Purposes has very recently considered whether a member of a Lodge may resign his membership under Rule 183 by e-mail and has given a ruling that he may do so, but the resignation only becomes effective when the Secretary receives a written confirmation bearing an original signature of the member; it then takes effect from the moment the Secretary received the e-mail message. If the Secretary has not received such written confirmation before the next regular meeting of the Lodge, he shall not report the resignation and the e-mail message shall be void.

There is an overriding proviso to the Rule, that if a Brother's resignation is communicated to the Lodge after he has been served with a notice to exclude him under Rule 181, it cannot be withdrawn, though the Lodge can still vote on the question of exclusion. If, however, the vote for exclusion is not taken, or fails to receive the requisite majority, the Lodge can then vote to give him twenty-one days to reconsider.

Exclusion

The other way in which a Brother's membership of a Lodge may be terminated is by his exclusion, usually for non-payment of his subscription, but sometimes for some other reason ("sufficient cause"). Exclusion is, in a sense, the converse of resignation: when a Brother resigns, he parts with the Lodge; when he is excluded, the Lodge parts with him.

Rule 148 provides that a Brother whose subscription to his Lodge remains unpaid for two full years ceases to be a member of it; the fact must be reported at the next regular meeting and recorded in the minutes. Though this is properly called "exclusion", it is often referred to as "cessation", to distinguish it from the process under Rule 181, which is also called exclusion ("cessation", no doubt, being regarded as a less harsh word than "exclusion"), but the distinction is illogical, since most Brethren excluded under Rule 181 are excluded for non-payment of subscriptions for a *lesser* period than two years, because the particular Lodge's by-laws permit it.

Rule 148 operates automatically and is actually as much to protect the Brother who is in arrears from running up further and further indebtedness as to protect his Lodge against its liability to pay Grand Lodge dues (and the Grand Charity contribution) in respect of him. By crystallising his liability, it therefore makes it easier for him to resume his Masonic career at some later date. No action is necessary on the part of the Lodge for the exclusion to take effect, and no action on the part of the Lodge can prevent it from happening; at midnight on the relevant date his membership comes to an end and, unless he is reinstated under Rule 182, it cannot be revived except by his becoming a rejoining member in accordance with Rule 163. A question that often arises is what constitutes a subscription being unpaid for two full years, and I am sorry to say that there is not, except in the simplest cases, unanimity of opinion as to the answer. In the straightforward case, a Brother may have paid his subscription up to 31 December 2006; thereafter he paid nothing to the Lodge; at midnight on 31 December 2008 his membership was automatically terminated. Such difficulties as occur most usually arise when a Brother who pays his subscription by Banker's Order fails to update the latter when the subscription is increased. The hard-line interpretation taken by some is that once the Brother has paid less than the full subscription for two years the Rule terminates his membership. The view, however, taken in the Grand Secretary's Office for many years is that until the accumulated arrears amount to two full years' worth of subscription at the rate current at the time, the Brother's membership continues. It is suggested that the latter approach is the correct one, not merely because it has been adopted by the

Grand Secretary's Office but because such ambiguity as exists should, in fairness, be resolved in favour of a Brother who would otherwise be penalised because of it.

When a Brother is to be excluded by vote for non-payment of subscription for a lesser period or for "sufficient cause", the procedure laid down in Rule 181 should be strictly followed. If it has not been, or the exclusion has taken place without due cause, the Grand Master or the relevant Metropolitan, Provincial or District Grand Master, as the case may be, may, under Rule 182, order his reinstatement – and suspend the Lodge if it fails to comply. He has the same powers if exclusion has occurred automatically under Rule 148. Such action may be taken either on his own initiative or on the complaint of the Brother excluded. Both the Lodge and the Brother have a right of appeal against the decision of a Metropolitan, Provincial or District Grand Master (though not of the Grand Master), but only if the Grand Registrar certifies that the decision is one that requires further consideration. It should be noted that the relevant Masonic authority *may*, but is not obliged to, order reinstatement. It is suggested that reinstatement should always be ordered if the cause is insufficient or the requisite majority has not voted in favour, [5] but that a reasonably robust view may be taken by Masonic authority of the procedural requirements if the Brother excluded cannot be said to have been prejudiced by a mere procedural defect.

As an example, the Rule requires notice to be served on the Brother concerned by registered post, which these days usually means recorded delivery with advice of receipt (see *Information for the Guidance of Members of the Craft*), but there have been instances of a Brother, who has refused to accept recorded delivery letters when aware of impending exclusion proceedings, but has received the full period of notice by first class post, attending the Lodge meeting to argue against his exclusion on the procedural or some other ground. In such an instance at least one Provincial Grand Master has refused to order reinstatement on the basis that the defect had not prejudiced the Brother and that the only effect of reinstatement would have been that the Lodge would have gone through the procedure again either with greater success or with similar evasive action on the Brother's part. The Rule gives no guidance as to what constitutes "sufficient cause", but clearly it must be something more than a merely frivolous reason. After non-payment of

---

5 The likely reason for the latter is that the Master or Secretary has failed to appreciate that Rule 181 requires a majority of two-thirds of the members *present*, not two-thirds of the members voting (see Chapter 4).

subscription the most common reason alleged is that a Brother's continued membership is causing disharmony in the Lodge. On more than one occasion recently an Appeals Court has held that the best proof that such an allegation is made out is that a sufficient number of Brethren have voted for exclusion.

Some of the fastidiousness over nomenclature mentioned earlier may stem from a failure to appreciate that exclusion, whether under Rule 148 or Rule 181, has essentially to do with *membership* rather than with *discipline*. For that reason it applies only to the particular Lodge and does not affect the Brother's membership of other Lodges or Orders – unless the Brother thereby becomes unattached. Occasionally one hears the cry, "It's disgraceful that he should be allowed to go through the Chair when he has been thrown out of another Lodge for not paying his subs" or "because they couldn't stand him". But such a statement betrays the fact that its utterer does see exclusion as a disciplinary matter, and wishes additionally to dictate to other Lodges whom they should or should not have among their members or their Officers. It is certainly reprehensible when a Brother fails to pay his subscription (though a fall-out between him and other members of the Lodge is not necessarily reprehensible on his part), but by so doing he places himself under a disability if he wishes to join another Lodge and that is a significant penalty in itself. Moreover, it is not always entirely the fault of the Brother who falls foul of Rule 148. Those of us who belong to several Lodges and other Masonic units are liable to lose track of what subscriptions may be outstanding (particularly because some Treasurers seem to have an aversion to Banker's Orders), and though the official line is that it is the duty of a Brother to seek out the Treasurer and pay him, we are grateful when he gives us a gentle (or even not so gentle) reminder that we are in default. If the Treasurer turns out to be incompetent or inefficient (such things have been!) we may find ourselves caught out by the Rule. For that reason, although Rule 148 imposes no requirement that the Secretary or the Treasurer should warn a Brother that he is in danger of being automatically excluded, simple courtesy requires that a warning should be given.

Voluntary resignation from the Craft

I have left to the end of this rather long chapter further consideration of voluntary resignation from the Craft under Rule 183A, which is comparatively rare and should certainly not be confused with resignation from a Lodge under Rule 183. Resignation from the Craft may be either for personal reasons or to avoid disciplinary sanctions. In either case the basic procedure is the same.

When a resignation is made in disciplinary circumstances, it takes effect as though the Brother had been expelled at the moment at which his resignation became effective. It is therefore final and irrevocable, since the Book of Constitutions provides no machinery for the readmission of someone who has been expelled. Whether a resignation is for personal or disciplinary reasons is determined by reference to the rather cumbersome test set out in Rule 183A(f). That paragraph of the Rule was introduced in 2006 to address the problem of a small number of persistent individuals who had resigned from the Craft to avoid almost certain expulsion and were unable to accept that having "kept their heads down" for a few (sometimes quite surprisingly few) years they should not allowed to resume full Masonic activity as though nothing had happened. The paragraph is comprehensive as well as cumbersome, and because – as just pointed out – there is no machinery for the readmission of someone who has been, or is deemed to have been, expelled, Brethren may be well advised not to resign under Rule 183A in disciplinary circumstances unless they are confident that they would otherwise be at risk of expulsion. It is undoubtedly the case that Brethren who have been convicted of even relatively minor offences – usually those involving dishonesty, violence or a sexual element – may find themselves under pressure to leave Freemasonry. This may come either from other members of their Lodge or Lodges (who may feel embarrassed by their presence among the members), or from the Provincial or District authorities (who will be thereby saved the very considerable amount of time and trouble that Masonic disciplinary proceedings can involve). The concerns of the members of the Lodge can, and should, be addressed by resignation under Rule 183, or exclusion from the Lodge under Rule 181 (though a surprising number of Lodges display a willingness to stand by their Brethren in time of adversity, which in many cases is commendable, though in serious cases it can only be regarded as perverse). Pressure from Masonic authority, however, may be more difficult to resist.

A Brother wishing to make use of the Rule (which he may do at any time) must complete the form prescribed by the Board of General Purposes (Form VR1), and return it together with his Grand Lodge Certificate and, if he is in the Royal Arch, Grand Chapter Certificate to the Grand Secretary. The latter has power, on receipt of a written request (but not otherwise), to dispense with the return of the Brother's Grand Lodge or Grand Chapter Certificate or compliance with any of the other specific conditions prescribed in the Rule. When all the conditions have been complied with to the satisfaction of the Grand Secretary, the resignation becomes effective and he will notify the former Brother. If the resignation is for personal reasons, the Brother may also complete a second form (VR2), which enables him to deposit clearance certificates with the Grand Secretary against the possibility that he may wish to resume his Masonic career at a later date.

4

VOTING AND ELECTIONS

...by a ready acquiescence in all votes and resolutions duly passed by a majority of the Brethren...

Charge after Initiation

Any democratic organisation depends on a system of voting so that the view of the majority may be ascertained. English Freemasonry has rather complex provisions, with different manners of voting and different majorities required for different purposes.

Grand Lodge

In the Grand Lodge, all matters are decided by a simple majority, with every Brother having one vote, except for the Grand Master or other Officer who presides, who has a second or casting vote in a case of an equal number of votes being cast on each side (Rule 59, Book of Constitutions). Each Brother votes by holding up one hand – by tradition the right hand, held parallel to the ground – and the result is then to be declared by the Officer presiding. Any two members of the Grand Lodge may demand that the votes be counted, and if the demand appears reasonable to the Officer presiding, the count is carried out under the direction of the Grand Director of Ceremonies.

In practice, the result of most votes is so readily apparent that it is not even declared by the Officer presiding. The Rule does make an exception for an election by ballot or voting papers, but as the only election now conducted in the Grand Lodge is that of the Grand Master, which has not been the subject of a contest for very many years, that exception may now be regarded as a dead letter. In 1986, when the Grand Lodge debated the removal of the penalties from the obligations, voting papers were prepared in case a count became necessary. In the event, the resolution for change was carried by a clear majority so that no count was called for. More recently, most notably in March 2003 when the formation of the

Metropolitan Grand Lodge of London was debated, preparations have been made for the Deputy Grand Directors of Ceremonies and Grand Stewards to act as tellers in case a count should be required.

Business to be brought before the Grand Lodge is set out in the paper of business for a Quarterly Communication which, together with the printed report of the previous Communication and any intervening meeting of the Grand Lodge, is to be sent out by the Grand Secretary at least ten days before each Quarterly Communication to those named in Rule 47. No business or motion may be brought before the Grand Lodge without notice on the paper of business, unless the Officer presiding allows it as being in his opinion urgent (Rule 42) or unless it is a motion to adopt or deal with a report or recommendation from a Board or Committee of the Grand Lodge (Rule 43). [1]

The paper of business for the Grand Lodge is settled by the Board of General Purposes, and any Brother wishing to bring any matter before the Grand Lodge must give notice to the Grand Secretary not less than seven days before the meeting of the Board at which the paper of business is to be settled (Rules 38 to 40). The Board has the power to reject any item as being inappropriate for any of the reasons set out in Rule 41. A more elaborate procedure is required under Rule 40 to alter the Rules in the Book of Constitutions or to change the general practice of the Craft (as, for example, by the removal of the penalties from the obligations in 1986), under which notice of motion must be given at one Quarterly Communication and the matter, together with any amendments of which due notice has been given, be voted on at the next.

Metropolitan, Provincial and District Grand Lodges
The Book of Constitutions is silent as to the method of voting in a Metropolitan, Provincial or District Grand Lodge. Accordingly, the same method of voting is to be used as in the Grand Lodge, unless the Metropolitan, Provincial or District by-laws make express provision.

Private Lodges
Paradoxically, the smallest Masonic units – Private Lodges – have by far the most complex array of voting provisions.

---

1   The exception under Rule 43 does not apply if the motion to adopt or deal with the report or recommendation would fall within the scope of Rule 40.

There are two ways of voting in a private Lodge: by show of hands and by ballot. Of these, voting by a show of hands is by far the more common. Unless a Rule in the Book of Constitutions or one of the by-laws of the Lodge requires it, a simple majority is all that is needed on a show of hands. Thus, at one end of the scale of importance, the minutes of the preceding meeting are confirmed by a simple majority, while at the other end of the scale, a decision by a Lodge to cease meeting and surrender its Warrant requires exactly the same majority. There are, however, several instances, either on a show of hands or on a ballot, where the Book of Constitutions requires a larger majority, which in some cases must be a majority of those *present*, rather than of those merely *voting*. It should not be overlooked that except when Rule 156 is called into play, there is no obligation on any member of a Lodge to exercise his vote.

Under no circumstances may a postal vote determine any question or matter. A Lodge's affairs may only be regulated by a vote of those present at a regularly summoned meeting. The result of any postal vote (or ballot) may be used only to give guidance to those present as to the views of those absent, and they should not feel themselves bound in any way to vote in accordance with the outcome of a postal vote. This is particularly so when the motion is put to the vote after a debate which "postal voters" will have had no opportunity of hearing.

Notice of motion

A question often arises as to the extent it is necessary to give notice of any intended resolution, either on the summons for the meeting at which it is to be put, or by way of notice of motion, whether orally or in writing, at the previous meeting. It is a view commonly held by many Brethren that virtually every resolution should be the subject of a notice of motion at the previous meeting. This, however, is by no means necessarily the case (and we have seen in the case of the Grand Lodge that generally a previous notice of motion is not required). In most matters it is quite sufficient that notice is given on the summons for the actual meeting at which the vote will be taken; and in the case of relatively insignificant matters, it may be reasonable enough for a resolution to be brought up on one of the Risings. If, however, a matter is one of potential significance to the Lodge, it should almost invariably be the subject of notice on the summons, whatever may be provided by the Book of Constitutions or the Lodge's by-laws, because (and not just as a matter of etiquette) it would be unfair to those Brethren who are absent to take a vote, without warning, on an important matter. This does not mean that a notice of motion needs to be given at the previous meeting; unless it is the practice (hardly more common these days than when the Rules in the Book of Constitutions were framed) to circulate the minutes soon after the meeting rather than with the summons for the next, only those Brethren present at the previous meeting could necessarily be expected to be aware of the notice, while for the remainder news of the notice of motion is likely to reach them simultaneously with the summons for the meeting at which the vote is to be taken. In this connection, however, it should be noted that a Lodge's by-laws may require that for some matters notice of motion should be given in writing on the summons for the previous meeting as well as on the summons for the meeting at which the resolution is to be put.

Voting by show of hands

Leaving aside any special provisions in individual Lodge by-laws, the Book of Constitutions requires a majority of two-thirds of the members *present* at a special meeting convened to decide whether a Lodge shall join a newly formed Grand Lodge in a territory where the Grand Master of the United Grand Lodge of England intends not to issue any Warrants for new Lodges in future (Rule 187). A majority of two-thirds of the members present and *voting* is required to change the place of meeting of a Lodge (Rule 141), and to effect the "block" transfer of membership from one Lodge to another on an amalgamation (Rule 165A). A majority of the members *present* is required to sponsor a new Lodge (Rule 94); to authorise the Master to displace one of his Officers (Rule 120) or to censure or exclude a Brother for the remainder of a meeting (Rule 180).

In all other cases a simple majority (*i.e.* of the members present and *voting*) is specified or implied: to sanction a Lodge of Instruction (Rule 132); to withdraw the sanction for a Lodge of Instruction (Rule 135); to adopt a Lodge's initial by-laws (Rule 136 – and, by by-law 11 of the current model set approved on behalf of the Grand Master, to amend the by-laws of a Lodge [2]; a resolution to permit cheques drawn on a Lodge's bank account to bear the signature of the Treasurer alone (Rule 153 – and, under the same Rule, for the election of the audit committee and for the approval of the Treasurer's accounts); a resolution to refer any matter to the Lodge's standing Committee or to appoint a Committee for a specific purpose (Rule 154); to regulate the Lodge's own proceedings (Rule 155); a resolution to seek a ruling under Rule 184 challenging the refusal of a certificate

---

2   It is important to check the by-laws of the individual Lodge on this point, as older by-laws may well require a larger majority or a more cumbersome procedure to be observed.

by the Grand Secretary under Rule 164(a) (see also Chapter 11); to desire a Brother to withdraw his resignation from a Lodge (Rule 183); and to dispose of a Lodge's property (other than its Warrant, books and papers, and Hall Stone Jewel, if any) upon dissolution (Rule 190).

Unless a ballot is required by a Rule of the Book of Constitutions or the Lodge's by-laws, a vote may be taken by a show of hands. Rule 155, however, clearly confers on the members of a Lodge the right to choose to resolve any question by ballot, and such a procedure may well be desirable in the event that there is a possibility that members may feel inhibited from voting according to their conscience or desire if a vote is taken openly.

In every case where a simple majority is required, in the event of an equality of votes (whether on a ballot or a show of hands) the Master in the chair or the Warden ruling the Lodge is *obliged* to give a casting vote (Rule 156).

Voting by ballot

A ballot may be conducted either by use of the ballot box or by means of ballot papers. The former is ideal for voting between two alternatives, typically "Yes" or "No"; the latter is appropriate for multiple choices. Ballot boxes come in various designs – including one ruled illegal by the Grand Lodge on the advice of the Grand Registrar, because it had been rigged to ensure that all ballots cast went into the same drawer! By far the most common is the two-drawer ("Yes" and "No") box. Such a ballot box may have either a single opening at the front, with a partition below it to direct the balls to one or other drawer, or an opening on either side, in which case the Brother balloting places one hand into each aperture, releasing the ball from whichever hand he has previously placed it in. Less common nowadays is the traditional single-drawer ballot box, which necessitates the use of a white ball and a black ball by each Brother voting, one ball being placed in the ballot box and the other in a bag, made of some suitably opaque material, brought round by one of the Deacons. This is, of course, the origin of the expression "to blackball". Such a method is not only more cumbersome, but increases the chance of the way that the Brother has voted being observed.

A paper ballot is used principally for the election of the Master and the Treasurer, but may be used in other situations where a choice lies between more than two options. It is inherently more open to abuse than voting by means of a ballot box because of the possibility of a brother's handwriting being recognised or of the ballot papers being marked in some way in advance. It is a regrettable fact that, although a ballot is intended to be secret, from time to time (and perhaps more often than we would care to admit) attempts are made to determine the identity of those who have cast a contrary vote.

The most common ballot is that for a candidate, whether for initiation, joining (or rejoining) or as an Honorary Member. The process being straightforward, it might be thought that there is little more to be said on the subject. Nothing could be further from the truth, as we shall see in a moment.

At its simplest, and under most circumstances, there will be little in the conduct of a ballot to tax the skill or intelligence of the Master of the Lodge. Except in the case of a ballot for an Honorary Member, before the ballot box is brought to him for examination, he should ensure that the Secretary reads out the certificate which he, the Master, will have *previously* signed at the foot of the third page of the Registration Form. If the ballot is for a candidate for initiation, there may be, in addition, a certificate from the Grand Secretary (if the candidate is unable to make the declaration on the second page of the Registration Form without qualification – see Chapter 11) or an adverse report under Rule 158. If there are two or more candidates for subscribing membership, it is perfectly appropriate for the ballot to be taken for them together.[3] In such a case it is sensible for the Master to announce to the Lodge prior to the ballot that the candidates will be balloted for together, and separately afterwards, if necessary. A joint ballot may be held even when one is a candidate for initiation and the other for joining; in the event that there are sufficient black balls to exclude, each candidate must then be balloted for individually (see *Information for the Guidance of Members of the Craft*).

If the normal two-drawer ballot box is used, the Master should check that both drawers are empty before the ballot box starts its journey round the Lodge. Although it is – regrettably – the almost universal practice, the Master would be well advised not to display the "No" drawer to the Brethren; if he feels the need of an independent witness, he should show the drawer just to the Immediate Past Master. If the ballot is for an Honorary Member, three black balls are required to exclude the candidate; otherwise the Lodge's by-laws may provide that instead of three, two black balls, or one black ball shall exclude (Rule 165). Before the ballot is taken, the Master should ensure that he is aware of the number of black balls required to exclude a candidate, so as to avoid a delay while he consults the by-

---

3   Honorary Members *must*, however, be balloted for separately from candidates for initiation or joining.

laws and thereby betrays the fact that there has been at least one adverse vote. When the ballot box has been carried around, the Master will again examine the "No" drawer. If the drawer is empty, no difficulty will arise, but the Master should again resist the temptation to show the drawer to the Brethren. The reason for this becomes apparent if there are any black balls in the drawer. Whether there are no black balls or the number of black balls is insufficient to exclude the candidate, the Master should declare only that the ballot is in favour of the candidate.[4] If the ballot is in the candidate's favour it is immaterial whether or not any adverse vote was cast, while displaying the drawer to the Lodge as a whole will disclose the fact of an adverse vote, or, worse, the Master may feel that it is incumbent on him to conceal any black ball or balls with his thumb. I remember an occasion when, in a Lodge where two black balls were required to exclude, the Master adopted just such an expedient to conceal a single black ball. When I took him to task privately afterwards, he said that he had always understood that the ballot should be declared as unanimous.

The difficulty arises when there are sufficient black balls in the drawer to exclude the candidate. In such a case the Master may perfectly properly declare that the ballot is against the candidate, and that will be the end of the matter for that occasion.[5] That is certainly the course he should take if the number of black balls is significantly greater than the number required to exclude a candidate. The Master may, however, with equal propriety order the ballot box to be taken round again in case some member has made a mistake in casting his ballot. I have on several occasions been told (usually in such a way as to imply a measure of approval on the part of the teller) the story, which I hope is apocryphal, of an occasion where there was a black ball in the box. When the Master announced the fact, one of the members stood up and said words to the effect of, "Worshipful Master, I am very sorry, but I am sure that I must have put my ball in the 'No' drawer by mistake." The Master was naïve enough to

---

4　Many Masters seem unable to avoid declaring that a vote or a ballot is "unanimous". The word must be one of the most misused in Freemasonry, as it should be used only when every single member of the Lodge present has voted the same way; usually the Master means that the vote was carried *nemine contradicente* (*i.e.* no one to the contrary, and usually abbreviated to *nem. con.*).

5　A rejected candidate may, of course, be proposed again – even at the very meeting at which he was rejected – but a Lodge may in its by-laws provide that a prescribed period must elapse before a rejected candidate may be again proposed (Rule 165).

take that statement at its face value and the candidate was initiated. If the story is true, the Master acted improperly in not sending the ballot box round a second time, whether or not the other member was telling the truth.

A far less common difficulty arises when the Master declares the ballot in favour of the candidate and one or more Brethren stand up and declare that they have cast a black ball. Where two or three black balls are required to exclude, this is more likely to happen after the meeting is over and Brethren compare notes. Assuming, however, that a single black ball excludes, and that the Brother declaring that he has cast it stands up in open Lodge, what happens next? Clearly the Master and the other Brother cannot both be telling the truth. It may be tempting for the Brethren as a whole to show their loyalty to their Master by accepting his word, or, worse, shouting down (in the nicest possible way) the other Brother. But that will not do. If the Master is not prepared to admit that he has been untruthful – or at least made a mistake, he should send the ballot box round again. If he does not do so, he risks a complaint being made to the Metropolitan, Provincial or District Grand Master with the resultant embarrassment both to himself and to the Lodge. If, on the other hand, the fact of an adverse ballot only becomes apparent after the meeting when Brethren compare notes, a complaint to the appropriate Masonic authority is the only course open to the Brethren whose votes have been disregarded.

If the ballot was for initiation and the initiation took place on the same night as the ballot, the Metropolitan, Provincial or District Grand Master is probably unable to do anything to affect the status of the candidate, since Rule 166 provides that, except for a Serving Brother, every candidate becomes a subscribing member of the Lodge upon being initiated in it; and, in any event, whether or not anything can be done to declare his membership void, the ceremony of initiation, once carried out, cannot be undone. He is, however, perfectly able to take appropriate disciplinary measures against any Brother whom he finds to have misbehaved. If, on the other hand, the ballot was for joining or rejoining membership, it is suggested that a Masonic authority, even if he does not have the power under the Rules in the Book of Constitutions to declare the election invalid, may perfectly properly ask the Brother concerned to resign on the grounds that the ballot was irregular.

Interestingly, in one recent instance a Lodge in a District took action against three Brethren who declared that they had cast adverse votes, on the grounds that they had thereby violated the secrecy of the ballot, which was a Masonic offence! This perverse decision was arrived at perfectly understandably on the basis of an incorrect statement contained in the book *Masonic Jurisprudence* by the late Bro. the Rev. J.T. Lawrence[6] brought about by a misreading – and a very inadequate summary – by the author of a case heard some years earlier in the Grand Lodge. There is undoubtedly very clear authority for the proposition that it is a Masonic offence to disclose how *another* Brother has voted, but none whatever for the proposition that a Brother may not disclose how *he himself* has voted, should he so desire. The earlier case heard in the Grand Lodge turned on the fact that the Brethren concerned, in disclosing how they had voted, had revealed that they had used the black ball from an improper motive (see also below).

Blackballing

There is a school of thought which holds that no candidate should ever be blackballed. This is a broad and general statement which has a small grain of truth lurking behind it, but should be treated with great caution and not taken literally on every occasion. It is a statement most commonly made by Brethren who wish to face down opposition to a candidate whom they have introduced. In fact, the position is a great deal more complex, and has given rise to several cases that have found their way before the Grand Lodge, prior to March 1964, or to an Appeals Court since that date.

Not every blackballing of a candidate, or threat to do so, is wrong. Etiquette, however, demands that the appropriate procedure should be followed when it is intimated that there may be an objection to a candidate. It is suggested that the following propositions would find general acceptance within the Craft.

A Lodge is essentially a group of Brethren who meet together to enjoy Freemasonry and each other's company. It therefore exists primarily for the benefit of its existing members, who have an interest in preserving its harmony, and only secondarily for the benefit of those who seek to become members. As has already been pointed out, Rule 165 of the Book of Constitutions provides that three black balls (or a lesser number specified in the by-laws) shall prevent the election of a candidate. This recognises that for the maintenance of harmony

---

6 This book, it is suggested, should be treated with very considerable caution, not only because its author was a clergyman rather than a lawyer, but also because it is now seriously out of date. Indeed, references to Rules in the Book of Constitutions are in some cases to Rules that no longer exist, or that were renumbered in the 1940 edition of the Book. It has been out of print for many years, and until very recently was becoming far less commonly met with than formerly. Unfortunately, the internet seems to be changing all that – and not for the better!

a candidate must be acceptable to all – or all but a very small number – of the members. It follows from this that the ballot is not intended to be a mere formality; it is to enable those who have a genuine objection to a candidate to express that view by casting a black ball. Most importantly, the right of every member of a Lodge to vote according to his conscience is not to be curtailed by reference to any supposed convention.

The freedom afforded by the ballot, with its accompanying secrecy, nevertheless carries with it the obligation for those who vote not to abuse their freedom. In a case before the Grand Lodge in March 1926, to which I shall refer again later, when a Brother had been excluded from his Lodge for threatening to blackball all future candidates in retaliation for others blackballing a candidate proposed by him, the Grand Registrar in advising the Grand Lodge said:

> "As I understand it, on the election of a candidate for initiation, or any other election, each Brother has a right to vote, and the right to vote, of course, implies a right to blackball. But that right must be exercised in good faith, and is capable of being abused, and the abuse of it may be a Masonic offence. The right is conferred on the understanding that it will be exercised in good faith, and in what are, or what the Brother honestly believes to be, the interests of the Craft in general and the Lodge in particular. Within these limits a Brother can vote as he pleases. He should not use the blackball wantonly or without some definite reason, and he must not do so merely to gratify some personal resentment or as a means of revenge for some real or supposed grievance. Still less must he do so in order to punish or injure some other Brother or Brethren, or to hinder the progress and prosperity of the Lodge. If he so uses the vote, he abuses the right, and is guilty of a breach of the trust imposed in him, and so commits a Masonic offence."

The blackballing of any candidate is a serious matter and is likely to reflect seriously on the candidate. It is therefore something to be avoided if at all possible. For that reason it is customary to give warning that a black ball may be cast. The current model by-laws for a Lodge have at the end a note as follows:

> *"Should there be any objection to the introduction of a Candidate for Initiation, or a Brother for Joining, it is recommended that such objection be mentioned privately to the Master or Secretary who may communicate with the proposer and give him the opportunity of withdrawing his Candidate."*

Those words are chosen carefully, and it is worth noting that the recommendation is, first, that the matter be mentioned privately; secondly, to use the Master or Secretary as a "cut out" between the objector and the proposer; and, finally, to give the proposer and seconder the opportunity of withdrawing the candidate. The recommendation is therefore not to be regarded as a means of "flushing out" opposition to a candidate with a view to applying pressure on the objector or objectors to withdraw all opposition.

Those who object to a candidate cannot, I believe, be compelled to give their reasons (and in some cases it may do far less damage to a candidate if reasons are not given), and provided they affirm that their objections are reasonable, and related to the particular candidate, they should not be accused of acting improperly. In the Grand Lodge in March 1926, the Grand Registrar, after the words quoted above continued:

> "He is not, of course, bound to disclose whether he voted, or how he voted, or why he so voted; but if it is proved that he deliberately misused the vote – if, for instance, he blackballs a Candidate, not because he has any objection to that particular Candidate, but in order to be revenged for some real or supposed grievance, or for some similar reason, or because he has resolved to blackball all Candidates, or all Candidates proposed by a particular Brother, and so to interfere with the efficient carrying on of the Lodge – he has, as I suggest to you, done that which will justify the interference of the Lodge, and even his exclusion by the Lodge."

Finally, it is not necessary for the candidate to be personally known to those who object to him, any more than it is necessary that he should be personally known to those who support him in the ballot; in both cases the tongue of report may have to suffice.

Ballots requiring a special majority

Although the election of the Master requires only a simple majority in the ballot, a motion – under Rule 105(b) – that the Master Elect be not installed requires a majority of three-quarters of the members *present* to be carried, and if passed the original election becomes void and the Brethren must forthwith elect another Brother as Master. The large majority required is an indication of the seriousness with which those responsible for framing the Rule regarded the displacement of a Master Elect; there is no matter on which a Lodge may vote which requires, under the Book of Constitutions, a more substantial majority.

A resolution to exclude a Brother permanently from a Lodge under Rule 181 requires a majority of two-thirds of the members *present*.

It will be observed that in either case the effect of requiring a special majority of the members *present* is to cause any abstention to be counted as a vote *against* the resolution. For this reason it is essential that the Master has an accurate count of the members present, so that he may calculate whether the votes cast in favour of the motion are sufficient; it is not enough merely to compare the number of balls in each drawer. The most common reason for excluding a Brother permanently is his failure to pay his subscription within the time specified in the Lodge's by-laws (Rule 148 provides that a lesser period than two years may be prescribed in a Lodge's by-laws, and Rule 181 used accordingly). The requirement of a special majority makes it difficult, if not well-nigh impossible, to use Rule 181 in a large Lodge, such as an Installed Masters' Lodge, where it is customary to confine a ballot to the Master and the Wardens. Unfortunately, there have from time to time been instances, either through ignorance on the part of the Master or Secretary, or through a deliberate disregard of the Rules, where members of large Lodges have been shown on an Annual Return as having been excluded from the Lodge when either no ballot has been taken or a unanimous vote of the Master and his Wardens has been assumed to be, or been treated as being, effective.

Election of Officers

Rule 105(a) of the Book of Constitutions provides that the Master is to be elected by ballot, and Rule 112(a) imports the same provision in respect of the election of Treasurer. In either case, the Brother receiving the largest number of votes of the members present and voting is elected. Since June 2004, however, it has been permissible, if certain conditions are satisfied, for the result to be declared without a ballot being held. The conditions are that (a) there is only one "nomination", (b) no other member qualified to be elected must have indicated to the Secretary that he wishes to be considered, (c) no member present calls for a ballot, and (d) notice must have been given on the summons of the intention to declare the ballot in favour of the "nominated" Brother. Unless all four conditions are satisfied, a paper ballot must be held. To make use of the abbreviated procedure, it is not necessary to have an express provision in the Lodge's by-laws (a spate of requests for changes to by-laws followed hot on the passing of the amendment to the Book of Constitutions) and, indeed, no such provision will be permitted. It is suggested that the appropriate formula for the summons might be either: "To declare, subject to Rules 105(a) and 112(a) of the Book of Constitutions, the ballot for Master and Treasurer for the ensuing year in favour of

Bro. *x* and Bro. *y* respectively. (Note: any member may demand a ballot.)" or "To elect a Master, Treasurer and Tyler for the ensuing year. (Note: the only nominations of which the Secretary is aware are of Bro. *x* as Master and Bro. *y* as Treasurer, and subject to the provisions of Rules 105(a) and 112(a) respectively it is proposed to declare the ballot in their favour. Any member may, however, demand a ballot.)". Though the second formula is longer, it is on the whole to be preferred.

To be qualified for election as Master, a Brother must be one who has served (or will by the time of Installation have served) for a full year in the office of Master, Senior Warden or Junior Warden in a regular Lodge *under the United Grand Lodge of England.* A full year is the period from one Installation meeting to the next Installation meeting at the corresponding period in the following year; so if the date of the first Installation was changed either by dispensation under Rule 139(c) or by the application of Rule 105(b), Rule 106 or Rule 108, or if the Lodge has, during the course of the year, changed its by-laws so that the *date* of the Installation meeting, but not the *meeting* in the annual cycle at which the Installation is held, falls earlier than in the previous year, a Warden who has served throughout the whole period is qualified.

Though it may seem unfair, a Brother who was invested as a Warden at the regular Installation meeting is qualified for election as Master even if he has not attended any other meeting during the year, whereas one who was absent at the Installation, but has attended and carried out his duties at every meeting since, is not qualified. If, however, a Brother has served part only of a year in a Warden's office, he may be rendered eligible to be elected Master by a dispensation granted by the Grand Master, or the Metropolitan, Provincial or District Grand Master, under Rule 109, but only on a petition giving the reason for the delay in his investiture, his actual service as a Warden and the special reason why a dispensation is sought. It should be particularly noted that a dispensation under Rule 109 may only be granted to render eligible a Brother who has *short* service in a Warden's office and not to render eligible a Brother who has *no* service as a Warden. It is also important to remember that a dispensation is required to render a Brother *eligible* for election, and it must therefore be granted before the day of election. This is in contrast to the dispensation which is required under Rule 115 to allow a Brother to be Master of two or more Lodges at the same time, which is only required after his election (since the need for it becomes apparent only at that point) and before installation.[7]

---

7   The same applies in the case of a dispensation under the same Rule to serve as Master of the same Lodge for more than two years in succession.

Any member of the Lodge, however junior, is qualified to be elected as Treasurer, the ability to perform the duties of the office and to safeguard the Lodge's assets being regarded as more important than having served in any qualifying office or achieved seniority in the Craft. It is as well at this point to mention that Brethren are commonly confused by the provisions of Rule 112(b) and assume that if the Treasurer dies or resigns, a successor cannot be elected without a dispensation given under that Rule. This is a misunderstanding of the Rule, and any such vacancy is to be filled under Rule 121 by election after due notice on the summons.[8]

The other Officer who is required to be elected is the Tyler (Rule 113). This may be done by a show of hands. The office of Tyler is the only one permitted to be held by a Brother who is not a subscribing member of the Lodge, and the office is generally so held. A Lodge may, however, resolve on the day of election that a subscribing member of the Lodge shall be Tyler without emolument, thereby allowing the Master to appoint the Tyler along with his other Officers. It should be noted that the Lodge may resolve only for the particular year, so that if it is the custom of the Lodge to have a subscribing member as its Tyler such a resolution must be passed annually. On no account will a by-law[9] be permitted requiring that a subscribing member shall be appointed as Tyler, as that would fetter the Lodge's ability to follow the normal practice of electing a non-member as Tyler.

---

8 For an explanation of Rule 112(b) and its application see Chapter 9.
9 A Metropolitan, Provincial or District Grand Master who purports to approve such a by-law on behalf of the Grand Master does so in excess of the authority conferred on him by Rule 136.

5

RANK AND PRECEDENCE, SEATING
AND SALUTING

...although distinctions among men are necessary to preserve subordination, yet ought no eminence of situation make us forget that we are Brothers...

First Lecture, Section 5

Just as with regalia, such disdain as many Masons profess for distinctions in Masonic rank is not necessarily borne out in practice. Brethren of the English Constitution may wear their distinctions in rank or status lightly, but it would be a mistake to assume that they are completely unaware of them – or wish others to be so either. The late Bro. Sir James Stubbs used to say that Brethren would kill for Grand Rank; and, on a lower level, one of the most unpleasant meetings I have attended in my entire Masonic career was of the Past Masters of a Lodge, which I had to chair as a very new Master, called to determine who should be put up for London Grand Rank. The Director of Ceremonies was the most senior active Past Master eligible and felt the rank to be his due, both for the work he had done and by order of seniority (often called "Buggins' turn"); the Secretary, only a year or so junior through the Chair, considered his own contribution to be the greater. Neither was prepared to concede an inch to the other.

This is not, however, a book on the psychology of the Masonic world; it is a factual work intended to give reliable guidance on etiquette and protocol. Even if individuals and Lodges choose to disregard such distinctions as may exist, they need to be, at least in outline, aware what those distinctions are. Much of the etiquette of Freemasonry lies in knowing when and how the rules may, or even should, be broken. But without first knowing what the rules are, an informed decision is impossible. There may be times when doing the wrong thing is right (or, conversely, doing the right thing is wrong), but those occasions, which are actually quite rare, should not be seen as justification for adopting a general policy of "anything goes". Moreover, for every instance when the wrong thing is right there will be many more when what only *seems* the wrong thing is right. Freemasonry and Freemasons being what they are, there is always likely to be someone to criticise or question all but the most obvious decisions – even if it is only, "Why on earth did he put *x* and not *y* next to the Master?" muttered somewhere in a corner. But the questions do not always stay in the corner, so that there may be instead a head-on confrontation: "How *could* you insult that Very Worshipful Brother by saluting the Provincial Junior Grand Warden before him?"

Another point to have in mind at all times is that where etiquette and practice are concerned there are often no absolutes, so that what is well-established custom in one Province may cause raised eyebrows in another.

Precedence

It might be thought that in order to determine who has precedence of whom, all that is necessary is to consult Rule 5 of the Book of Constitutions, in the case of Grand Officers, and Rule 71 – together with the Schedule to Rule 68(a) – in the case of Provincial or District Grand Officers. If only it were so simple! On most occasions both of those two Rules have to be read in conjunction with each other, but on some occasions only one is relevant. Thus only Rule 5 is relevant for determining the precedence in processions into and out of the Grand Lodge, and only Rule 71 in the same situation in a Provincial or District Grand Lodge. In each case the personal rank of each individual is ignored and his precedence is determined exclusively by the office he holds or is occupying temporarily as a holder of the past rank standing in for an absentee.[1]

Rule 5 applies throughout the whole of the English Constitution, but the order of precedence laid down in Rule 71 applies only within the Province or District concerned. Outside their own territory those Provincial or District Grand Officers who are not also Grand Officers are numbered among those who are named last in the order of precedence in Rule 5 ("The Master, Past Masters qualified under Rule 9, and Wardens of the Grand Stewards' Lodge, and of every other private

---

1   As a matter of practice, in the Grand Lodge only those Officers for whom there is no Deputy or Assistant – or these are themselves absent – are substituted for in this way, and a Deputy or Assistant "acting up" acquires no additional precedence as a result.

Lodge.") The same applies to the holders of Metropolitan Ranks.[2] Within the Grand Lodge, except for processions (see above), precedence is exactly as determined under Rule 5, so that a Past Master of great seniority who has never been promoted out of light blue will outrank (for what it is worth) a newly appointed Assistant Provincial Grand Master who is not a Grand Officer – even though the latter wears a chain! – and the present Master of a Lodge will outrank both.[3] Away from the meetings of the Grand Lodge precedence will shift according to the location.[4] A good way of looking at this is to regard the English Constitution, where rank is regulated overall by Rule 5, as containing a number of local "pockets" – 47 in the Provinces and 31[5] in Districts abroad – where the precedence of those, other than Grand Officers, having rank *within them* is regulated by Rule 71, and that of those who do not by Rule 5. The latter do not

---

2   The only apparent exceptions to this are to be found in the Groups, formed under Rule 91 out of some (but not all) of the Lodges abroad not falling under any District, where *all* holders of each of the Overseas Ranks have precedence amongst themselves, according to their respective dates of appointment. This can lead to anomalies, as when, say, a holder of Overseas Grand Rank from outside a Group attends a meeting of a Lodge within the Group and is entitled to take precedence over a respected Brother whose appointment to that rank was more recent. Such cases may be among those where, to avoid ruffling feathers unnecessarily, etiquette – or at any rate expediency – dictates that "doing the wrong thing" is actually right.

3   I had not long written this when the editor of the London Grand Rank Association Bulletin sought my advice on a question he had been posed for the Bulletin's *General Tips* column. On a cruise, where a Masonic cocktail party was held, it was necessary to elect the most senior Brother as President; how did Senior London Grand Rank and London Grand Rank correspond to Provincial ranks? On the high seas, only Rule 5 can apply, so that in the absence of a Grand Officer or a Past Grand Steward, the most senior is the Brother who, being currently Master of a Lodge, was installed first or, if there is none, the Brother who has been a Past Master for longest. (As between two Brethren installed on the same day, if it is impossible to determine the time of installation, Rule 5 clearly implies that the Master of the Lodge with the lower number should have priority.) This answer has probably given offence to an incalculable number of Provincial Grand Wardens and holders of Senior London Grand Rank, but I stand by it.

4   The only exceptions (where Rule 5 applies in all its rigour) are the five Lodges in London which have been excluded from the Metropolitan Area and therefore remain under the direct authority of the Grand Master: The Grand Stewards' Lodge, the three Time Immemorial Lodges, and Royal Alpha Lodge, No. 16 (the Grand Master's private Lodge of which no one becomes a member without the Grand Master's approval).

5   Two of these, Burma and Pakistan, are currently dormant.

lose their rank, but they cannot claim precedence (see also below). As those within the local "pocket" will, however, almost invariably constitute the great majority at any particular meeting, few major problems are likely to arise.

In the two "pockets" comprising the Metropolitan Area of London and those Lodges abroad which do not fall under Districts, different rules apply. There the holders of Metropolitan (*i.e.* London) or Overseas Ranks take seniority within each grade from the order of their appointment to the rank. In London, the Metropolitan Grand Officers – unless present in an official capacity, when they wear aprons bearing the emblems of their respective offices and rank in the order set out in the Appendix – are no more than holders of either Senior London Grand Rank or London Grand Rank (the Appendix shows which). Unless, therefore, he is a Grand Officer, the Metropolitan Senior Grand Warden will on an *ordinary* occasion rank behind the most junior of the previous year's batch of holders of Senior London Grand Rank.

Despite the fact that Provincial and District Grand Officers and holders of Metropolitan and Overseas Ranks cannot claim precedence outside their respective areas, there has certainly been a growing trend over a considerable number of years to accord at least a measure of recognition of those ranks in other places. This is emphatically a matter of *etiquette*, and a particularly sensitive one, since there is so much local variation. Some Provinces have gone so far as to amend the standard toast list at dinner (see Chapter 13), while others have insisted on adherence to the letter of the Rules in the Book of Constitutions. Local policy will therefore affect the procedure which is adopted in an individual Lodge on seating, saluting and any outgoing procession, as well as the toast list at the after-proceedings.

Leaving aside the position under the Book of Constitutions (though the choice of words "cannot *claim* precedence" is interesting), there are reasons both for and against a more relaxed policy. There is a general feeling that "dark blue is dark blue" wherever it comes from, and this was certainly an attitude that prevailed in many (but by no means all) London Lodges in the days when the number of appointments to London Grand Rank was much more tightly restricted than it is now.[6] In such Lodges a Brother who already had a Provincial rank would often let it be known that although he was eligible, he did not wish to be considered for recommendation as that would delay the promotion of

---

6   One appointment each year for every three London Lodges until 1978, with a typical wait
    of twelve to fifteen years after coming out of the Chair – and in many cases even longer.

those who belonged only to a London Lodge. On the other hand, there is no doubt that in some Provinces a more generous policy is applied to Provincial Ranks than in others, both as to the length of "time through the Chair" required and the level of rank awarded, so that if all those wearing dark blue are indeed equal, some are more equal than others. Etiquette demands that a Brother "out of his area" accepts with equal grace either recognition of his rank elsewhere or the strict position under the Book of Constitutions, while the Lodge (or its Director of Ceremonies), unless a strict policy has been laid down by the Provincial authorities, should be prepared to err on the side of generosity at least in the case of a visitor with one of the more senior ranks. What is unacceptable behaviour is (as happened to me once) for a visitor who was a holder of London Grand Rank to complain rather aggressively in the bar before dinner that a neighbouring Provincial Grand Master had laid down that holders of London Grand Rank had no precedence in his Province, and then when told that the Provincial Grand Master was perfectly correct in so doing, to pitch into me and "Grand Lodge" for allowing it to happen.

Now for one or two traps – or popular misconceptions that need to be dispelled. There are some who believe that *any* Grand Officer of the year (which in the United Grand Lodge of England's terms means a present Grand Officer – *i.e.* one of those appointed annually under Rule 18)[7] takes precedence ahead of all Past Grand Officers, however senior. A cynic might say that this is a myth put about mainly by the holders of the less exalted offices in the Grand Lodge who, buoyed up by the undoubted cachet of having an acting, rather than a past, rank and the fact that they wear a chain in the Grand Lodge, are anxious to secure the maximum benefit from their year of glory. This is most likely a slur upon such Brethren, but, human nature being what it is, some of them are not always swift to disabuse others of the idea. The misconception probably has its roots, first, in the fact that Grand Officers of the year, if they are visitors to a Lodge, are invariably (almost "as of right") included in the procession of one of the Rulers when he attends a meeting, whereas Past Grand Officers rarely are; and, secondly, in the fact that a Provincial or District Grand Master may send one of his Provincial or District Grand Officers, present or past (but more usually present),

---

7   In at least one Province the expression is used to mean a Grand Officer who was appointed or promoted to a past, as well as one appointed or promoted to an acting, rank at the most recent annual Investiture of the Grand Lodge.

to visit any of his Lodges ("to represent him", as it is commonly described), who is to be placed on the immediate right of the Brother presiding – and the idea thereby becomes established in the minds of some Brethren that it is the active rank, rather than the representative capacity that gives the Brother his precedence.

Rule 5 is quite clear on the matter: the order in which the members of the Grand Lodge rank is strictly laid down, and the Rule provides that as between two or more holders of the same rank seniority is determined according to the order in which they were appointed to that rank. This applies even within a single Annual Investiture of the Grand Lodge, where the Grand Officers of the year are invested first, then those existing Grand Officers receiving promotions to Past Grand Ranks, and finally those receiving a Past Grand Rank for the first time. Thus of those receiving the same level of appointment (either active or past) on the same day the order of seniority is, *and will for ever thereafter remain*: first those appointed to active office, secondly those *promoted* to the corresponding past rank, and finally those *first appointed* to the corresponding past rank. Additionally, those with an active office, so long as they hold that office, rank ahead of all those with the corresponding past rank; for them past rank follows automatically on the termination of the active office, and is not conferred separately at the end of the term. Within each category also, Brethren rank according to the order in which they were invested – generally, but not always, alphabetical order.

In Provinces and Districts, where seniority is regulated by Rule 71, exactly the same applies; even though it is not explicitly stated that those currently in office precede holders of past ranks or that within a rank Brethren take their seniority from the order in which they were appointed, any other arrangement would be a nonsense. The position is, however, complicated by the fact that in some Provinces and Districts the order of investiture is: active offices, followed by past ranks, and finally promotions, instead of the order adopted by the Grand Lodge. It is suggested that such an order is illogical, as it accords priority to those receiving rank for the first time rather than those being given a further reward for continuing effort.

Because of the need on the part of the Grand Director of Ceremonies, his Deputies and Assistants, as well as their Metropolitan, Provincial and District counterparts, to establish precedence between Grand Officers, the *Masonic Year Book* published by the Grand Lodge shows the holder of an office in a particular year as, for example, "AGStB 55" (as opposed to "PAGStB 55") for ever after, even though at the end of his term he automatically became PAGStB and should thereafter be so described. Unfortunately, it being impossible to devise a method of showing ranks which at least someone will not misunderstand, some of these Brethren, as well as others who misunderstand the convention adopted, have been known to insist that their rank remains as designated in the Year Book (*i.e.* "AGStB").

It should be clear by now that rank and precedence, though often producing the same result, are not the same thing. Many of the conundrums which can cause perplexity to Directors of Ceremonies and others are quite easily resolved by drawing a clear distinction between rank and precedence. For this purpose the analogy of "pockets" used above may be carried a little further: within each "pocket" there is a smaller "pocket" which contains the local Rulers who take precedence over those who fall within the larger "pocket". The smaller "pocket" is expanded from time to time to include a Provincial or District Grand Officer representing the Provincial or District Grand Master. By way of illustration, outside his Province an Assistant Provincial Grand Master takes his chance according to his *rank* under the Grand Lodge, but within his Province, even if he is not a Grand Officer, he has *precedence* even of a visiting Provincial Grand Master. Similarly, a Provincial or District Grand Officer – typically one of the Wardens – "representing" the Provincial or District Grand Master has the same precedence as the latter would enjoy if present, even over the Deputy or Assistant Provincial or District Grand Master (though in a well-conducted Province or District, affairs should be so arranged that such a conflict never arises in practice).

Another trap for the unwary or unprepared Director of Ceremonies is the presence at a meeting of a present or past Grand Steward. The former is more straightforward than the latter: a present Grand Steward ranks as a Grand Officer – after Past Assistant Grand Pursuivants and before the Grand Tyler. But even so there may be a catch. The office of Grand Steward is greatly sought after, and it is rare for each year's Board of nineteen Grand Stewards not to include at least one Brother who is already a Grand Officer and who will therefore have a higher personal rank – sometimes as high as Provincial Grand Master, or even, on occasion, Past Pro or Deputy Grand Master – and if such a Brother has elected to exercise his legitimate choice of regalia in favour of red rather than dark blue, his status could be overlooked. Past Grand Stewards are almost invariably a source of great confusion to those – the great majority of Brethren – who do not understand their precedence. Although a present Grand Steward ranks as a Grand Officer, a past one does not; he does, however, rank one place (but what a difference that one place makes) above "The Master, Past Masters qualified under Rule 9, and Wardens of the Grand Stewards' Lodge, and of every other private Lodge" in the order of precedence laid down in Rule 5. In other words, he precedes all Provincial or District Grand Officers or holders of Metropolitan or Overseas Ranks other than a Brother entitled to demand admission under Rule 122, or one sent to represent the Metropolitan, Provincial or District Grand Master.

A visitor from a recognised Constitution is *entitled* to no precedence, but as a *courtesy* he is generally treated as though he held the corresponding rank or office under this Constitution. If more than one Constitution is represented, under the United Grand Lodge of England (unlike many other Constitutions) foreign visitors take precedence according to the seniority of their respective Grand Lodges, not according to the seniority of the rank held by the Brother himself.

Seniority in a Lodge of Joining Past Masters

When a Past Master joins a Lodge he takes seniority immediately after the junior Past Master at the time his membership becomes effective (as does a Past Master of the Lodge who, having resigned, subsequently rejoins it); if he is currently serving for the first time as Master of any Lodge, he takes seniority after the Brother who is the junior Past Master at the time when he himself becomes a Past Master. It should be noted that the same applies to a pre-existing member of the Lodge who attains the status of Installed Master through another Lodge.

In recent years the relative seniority of Past Masters has become something of an issue with the advent of formal amalgamations of Lodges under Rule 102A. Interestingly, the order of seniority set out in the previous paragraph is nowhere directly laid down in the Book of Constitutions but rests upon a single ruling of the Board of General Purposes, on the subject of a rejoining Past Master, set out in *Information for the Guidance of Members of the Craft*. If the ruling is followed strictly, the Past Masters of the Amalgamating Lodge or Lodges in the amalgamation take their seniority after the junior Past Master at the time they transfer their membership to the continuing Lodge. As an amalgamation is intended to effect the fullest possible merger of the Lodges participating in it into a single unit, it will be seen that the ruling "sells short" the Past Masters of Amalgamating Lodges (and sells even shorter the Brother who is Master of the continuing Lodge at the time of the amalgamation, as he will have a number of Past Masters interposed between him and his predecessor). Although a ruling of the Board of General Purposes should not be disregarded, it has less authority than an edict of the Grand Lodge. Because the ruling was given long before formal amalgamations came into existence, it is suggested that until the Board either affirms that its ruling applies to amalgamations or varies it, etiquette dictates that for the Past Masters of and in a Lodge that is the result of an amalgamation the two or more lines of Past Masters should be "dovetailed" together according to the date of their respective Installations; this might be best and most elegantly exemplified on a summons by showing parallel lists of Past Masters down to the date of the amalgamation and a single list thereafter.

Seating

As a basic rule, *Seating follows Precedence*. This is invariably true of the best seats, and in other cases if it does not apply there will be a compelling reason. This single rule will generally be all that a Lodge Secretary or Director of Ceremonies needs to know. If the occasion is likely to be one of greater complexity, there will almost inevitably be a guest of honour attending who will be accompanied by the Metropolitan, Provincial or District Grand Director of Ceremonies or one of his Deputies or Assistants. It should be assumed that such a Brother knows what he is about – and even if he manifestly does not, it will generally be as well to pretend to believe that he does. On no account should he be argued with publicly. This is a matter not only of etiquette but of elementary self-preservation.

An occasion does not need to become very elaborate before two additional rules come into play: *Seating follows Function* and *Seating follows Access*. In other words practicability must sometimes override precedence.

When one of the Rulers of the Craft visits a Provincial Grand Lodge and installs a new Provincial Grand Master he is normally attended by at least three, and often four, Directors of Ceremonies – typically the Grand Director of Ceremonies and his three Deputies. All of these are seated at the east end of the front row of seats on the north side of Provincial Grand Lodge, while the Provincial Grand Director of Ceremonies and his team sit facing them on the south side. Here, therefore, seating follows function. The Grand Secretary (or Assistant Grand Secretary) is present to read out the new Provincial Grand Master's Patent of Appointment as soon as the latter has been escorted into Provincial Grand Lodge, and a Chaplain is present to deliver a prayer. These two Brethren are normally seated at the north and south ends respectively of the front row of the dais (unless their personal ranks secure them seats closer to the centre) – a case of seating following function, but also a case of seating following access, because there is no point in these Brethren being tucked away in the second or third row, where they cannot be seen. Finally the Grand Officers in the Ruler's procession will need seats on the dais which they can get into and out of easily, almost certainly in some cases out of their strict order of precedence, so that here again seating follows access.

When one of the Rulers of the Craft visits a Lodge, unless it is a very private visit indeed, he takes with him a Director of Ceremonies, perhaps the Grand Director of Ceremonies, but more usually a Deputy or Assistant Grand Director of Ceremonies. Such a Brother is seated at the extreme east end of the front row on the north side of the Lodge, in the place normally occupied by the Senior Deacon, who moves a place to the west (perhaps more, depending on whether the Metropolitan, Provincial or District authorities are present or represented, and if so where their Director of Ceremonies is customarily seated).

All this will be mirrored to a greater or lesser extent in London, Provinces and Districts. Except in relation to Grand Lodge's practice, definitive guidance is impossible in a work of this nature, since practice varies widely between individual Provinces and Districts, though in the Metropolitan Area of London the Grand Lodge practice is closely followed. Indeed, different practices can prevail in different places even within an individual Province or District. It is always a mistake to assume that something is wrong just because it is different.

A question occasionally arises as to the seating of distinguished visitors from other Constitutions. As already explained, a visitor from a recognised Constitution is *entitled* to no precedence. Nevertheless, as a *courtesy* he should be seated in a place commensurate with his rank. In the Grand Lodge, distinguished visitors from other Grand Lodges are seated behind the Grand Chaplain, to the left of the Throne, and this is a useful example to follow in a Private Lodge: by seating such Brethren to the left of the Chaplain on the south side of the Master it is possible to avoid any direct conflict in precedence of seating between them and a Metropolitan, Provincial or District hierarchy, whose members will naturally be seated to the Master's right.

The length of the discussion in the first section of this chapter on rank and precedence might suggest otherwise, but it will be seen from this section that the Rules in the Book of Constitutions lay a very light touch on how such things translate into reality in an actual Lodge.

Saluting

Nowhere in the Book of Constitutions is it laid down that salutes shall be given. Rule 6 (to which reference should be made in cases of doubt) prescribes that when salutes are given they shall be as there set out, but the Rule gives no guidance at all on when they should be given. Here, as in other matters, local practice varies enormously, so that the practice even of one Lodge meeting in a particular Masonic Hall may be totally alien to another Lodge meeting there.

Divisions of opinion exist on the extent to which salutes are necessary or desirable at each meeting. They are not necessary at all, except to conform to the general or local practice when a Ruler or one representing him pays a formal visit. In many Lodges, particularly those with a high proportion of Grand Officers among their members, no salutes are ever given except on those occasions, but in most Lodges many Brethren would feel cheated if such a minimalist policy were the norm.

In the Grand Lodge, at each Quarterly Communication, only the Officer presiding is saluted, immediately after the Grand Lodge has been opened (except if the Grand Master is present in March, when his salute is deferred until he has been proclaimed following his re-election). At the Annual Investiture, however, each of the Rulers is saluted immediately after he has been proclaimed, and after all the new Grand Officers have been invested salutes are given in turn to the newly invested and other Right Worshipful Brethren present, then to the newly invested and other Very Worshipful Brethren, and finally to the newly invested and other Grand Officers. This will be mirrored to a greater or lesser extent at the Annual Communications of Provincial and District Grand Lodges, with the added complication of having to "interleave" Grand Officers with the Provincial or District hierarchy, according to the local custom.

When one of the Rulers of the Craft installs a new Provincial Grand Master, he enters Provincial Grand Lodge after it has been opened (either by the Deputy Provincial Grand Master in Charge or, if the latter is the Provincial Grand Master designate, by another senior Brother in the Province) and, having accepted the gavel, occupies the Chair. (It should be noted that if one of the Rulers of the Craft is the principal person present at a Metropolitan, Provincial or District Grand Lodge or any Private Lodge, he *only* occupies the Chair if he is about to carry out a ceremony of Installation. *On all other occasions* he takes the seat to the immediate right of the Brother presiding.) Having appointed the two most senior Metropolitan, Provincial or District Grand Masters to act as his Wardens[8] and another Brother (generally one in holy orders) to act as Chaplain, he is saluted according to his rank. In the course of the ceremony, as soon as the new Provincial Grand Master has been installed, the Wardens and Chaplain are replaced and the

---

8   Unless the actual Grand Wardens are *both* present (see Rules 29 and 122).

Provincial Grand Master is proclaimed and then saluted with seven by all except the Installing Officer. The Deputy Provincial Grand Master is then installed, but when he is proclaimed and saluted only the Brethren of the Province are called upon to stand. The same procedure is adopted for the reappointed and for the newly appointed Assistant Provincial Grand Master(s). This procedure appears to have been adopted to get round the problem of senior Brethren from other Provinces having been in the past reluctant, or at any rate uncertain whether, to stand and salute Brethren whom they personally outrank.

In a Private Lodge much will depend on the particular occasion. One of the Rulers of the Craft attending formally will be saluted immediately after entry and thereafter no further salutes will be given. If, for example, the Provincial Grand Master is also present, the Ruler will come in after (or, as it is sometimes put, "on top of") him, so that as many Provincial salutes as are desired can be given before he arrives. Another Grand Officer standing in for a Ruler on a special occasion, and therefore accompanied by a Director of Ceremonies, will also be saluted immediately after entry. A Grand Officer visiting officially (*i.e.* on behalf of the Grand Master) on a lesser occasion, unaccompanied by a Director of Ceremonies, will be saluted immediately before the Risings (or before the closing if it is an emergency meeting) and it is then at the discretion of the Lodge's Director of Ceremonies whether the other Grand Officers are saluted. On ordinary occasions Grand Officers and others will be saluted, if at all, at whatever point is the custom of the Lodge (and in many it is the custom not to salute a Grand Officer who is a member unless other Grand Officers are present). In many London Lodges, that used to be, and still is, immediately before the Risings; in others it was, and still is, on the first Rising (and holders of Metropolitan ranks on the second Rising); in most Provincial Lodges it is earlier in the meeting, usually after the minutes have been confirmed.

A plethora of Grand Officers, Provincial or District Rulers and other Provincial or District Grand Officers can tax even a Provincial or District Grand Director of Ceremonies' skills. Here, as with seating, as a general rule *the order of saluting follows precedence*, but there are exceptions (see below). A second rule is that a Brother is only saluted by those of whom he has precedence (who may be all or almost all of those present) or whom he outranks. Thus a Provincial Grand Warden is saluted as the Provincial Grand Master's representative by all present, including Grand Officers, but if Grand Officers are also saluted, he must join in the salute to them. A third rule is that categories of salutes should not be mixed; even if two categories attract the same number of salutes, it is wrong to conjoin them.

Applying these rules, and assuming a Lodge in a Province, at which there is such a plethora as mentioned above, the Provincial Grand Master is saluted with seven, then the Deputy, if present, with five, then the Assistant(s) separately from the Deputy with five. At this point a mild illogicality sets in. A past Deputy or Assistant Provincial or District Grand Master who has served two or more years in office retains his entitlement to five salutes within his Province or District, although he no longer has any precedence other than that to which his personal rank entitles him. This is the *logical* point at which to give such salutes if such a Brother is present, but there is no clue given in Rule 6, which covers these salutes in a footnote, on the question of from whom they are entitled to receive them. It is suggested that only those Brethren whom they outrank as Grand Officers should take part in the salutes, but an even neater solution is for the Director of Ceremonies to call on only Brethren of the Province to stand (rather as at a Provincial Installation – see above), thereby avoiding any conflict in most cases.[9] Thereafter Right Worshipful Brethren are saluted, followed by those who are Very Worshipful, then the remaining Grand Officers and, finally, the Provincial Grand Officers. A Grand Steward ranks as a Grand Officer during his year of office and is therefore saluted as such. No salutes, paradoxically, are given to Past Grand Stewards, even though they rank ahead of Provincial Grand Officers.

A foreign visitor is not entitled to any salutes, however senior he may be in rank. As a matter of courtesy, however, he is accorded the salutes to which his rank would entitle him under this Constitution, but only *after* all the salutes to English Brethren have been given.

---

9 Another solution is to omit these salutes altogether, but this may not be well received by those to whom they apply.

6

PROCEDURES

155. The members present at any Lodge duly summoned have an undoubted right to regulate their own proceedings, provided they are consistent with the general laws and regulations of the Craft; but a protest against any resolution or proceeding, based on the ground of its being contrary to the laws and usages of the Craft, and for the purpose of complaining or appealing to a higher Masonic authority, may be made, and such protest shall be entered in the Minute Book if the Brother making the protest shall so request.

Rule 155, Book of Constitutions

On the face of it, Rule 155 allows very considerable latitude to individual Lodges to conduct their affairs as they wish. And so to some extent it does, but "the laws and usages of the Craft" are themselves quite extensive and constitute a significant check on the apparent latitude conferred (or, perhaps more accurately, declared) by it. Nonetheless, the provisions of the Rule should be borne in mind while reading this chapter, which sets out to record current protocol and practice, not to lay down rigidly procedures which must be followed.

The Warrant

The Warrant of Constitution is the authority under which the Lodge meets. It is handed on from one Master to another, each of whom is, during his term of office, charged with its safe custody on behalf of the Grand Master and is obliged by Rule 101 to produce it at every meeting of the Lodge. Most Masters delegate this to the Secretary or the Tyler (who will put the Warrant away in the Lodge box or locker), but if the Warrant should be lost or mislaid, the Master is the one who is answerable for their default.

In many Lodges the obligation on the part of the Master to *produce* the Warrant at each meeting has been misinterpreted as an obligation to unfold and display it:

("Brethren, as required by Rule 101 of the Book of Constitutions, I display the Warrant of the Lodge" – sometimes, indeed, merely raising in the air the leather case which is to be presumed to contain the Warrant). The obligation of the Master in this respect extends only to ensuring that the Warrant is brought into the Lodge Room for the duration of the meeting. The Warrant is required to be *displayed* to a candidate at his initiation and on its being handed over to the new Master at his Installation. Occasionally one sees a Centenary Warrant being displayed or transferred at this point, because the Master (or the Secretary or Director of Ceremonies) has incorrectly assumed that the Centenary Warrant supersedes the Warrant of Constitution.[1]

Four Lodges alone have the privilege of working without a Warrant: The Grand Stewards' Lodge and the three Time Immemorial Lodges.

Opening in all three degrees

In some Lodges it is the custom to open the Lodge in all three degrees, before resuming in the first degree, irrespective of what ceremony, if any, is due to be worked. This is a matter of individual choice for such Lodges and there is nothing objectionable in the practice (though it does add to the length of a meeting, and may be regarded by some as *undesirable* on that account). For a Lodge that adopts this procedure it is equally legitimate to keep Entered Apprentices and Fellow Crafts out of the Lodge until it has been resumed in the first degree, or to ask such Brethren to retire before the Lodge is opened in each successive degree. Nonetheless, the members of a Lodge that adopts the former procedure might ask themselves whether the small saving of time thus achieved genuinely compensates for the way in which the junior Brethren are precluded from seeing the opening of the Lodge until they have been raised.

Dispensations

As a general rule, a dispensation should be read immediately before the proceeding which it authorises. The notable exception to this is any dispensation that authorises the holding of the meeting itself – whether on a different date or at a different place or as an emergency meeting – which must be read immediately

---

1 A Centenary Warrant is the authority for the members of the Lodge to wear the Centenary Jewel, and a Bi-Centenary Warrant is a similar authority to wear a Bi-Centenary Bar on the ribbon of the Centenary Jewel. Neither has any further function.

after the Lodge has been opened and before any business is transacted (*not* before the Lodge is opened, as I have occasionally seen suggested). A dispensation is a means of permitting or regularising something that is normally forbidden by the Rules in the Book of Constitutions, and may be granted either prospectively or, less frequently, retrospectively (when it is called a dispensation *nunc pro tunc* – literally meaning "now for then" – and, if it is issued by the Grand Master, costs twice as much as an ordinary prospective dispensation, to compensate for the additional work entailed in the Grand Secretary's Office). There is no general power to grant a dispensation, and even the Grand Master may therefore only do so if a particular Rule in the Book of Constitutions allows it. Certain dispensations may be granted only by the Grand Master; others may in a Metropolitan Area, Province or District be granted by the Metropolitan, Provincial or District Grand Master (and generally, under the terms of his Patent of Appointment, by a Grand Inspector in his Group – Rule 91). For historical reasons, which are now largely obsolete because of the speed of modern methods of communication, certain dispensations which in London or a Province would have to be granted by the Grand Master may be granted by the District Grand Master.

Deaths

It is customary to deliver a tribute to a deceased Brother and then stand for a few moments in silence[2] at the beginning of the meeting. This is generally done immediately after the Lodge has been opened and any necessary dispensation has been read, but before the minutes are confirmed. Custom does, however, vary, and there may be special reasons on a particular occasion to defer it until after the minutes. In most Lodges it is the practice to place the Brother's name within a black-edged box at the head of the agenda; some print the summons on such an occasion in black throughout, and a few still place a black border round the front page. It is interesting to note, in this connection, the instructions given to the Craft on the death of the late MW Bro. Lord Farnham, Past Pro Grand Master, in 2001:

---

2   In some Lodges the Organist will play quiet music at this point (the hymns "The Lord's my shepherd" *(Crimond)*, "Abide with me" *(Eventide)* and "The day Thou gavest, Lord, is ended" *(St. Clement)* are probably the most common). As some Brethren feel strongly that complete silence should be observed, a visiting Organist will be well advised to ascertain the custom of the Lodge beforehand from the Master or the Director of Ceremonies.

"In consequence of the lamented death ... of MW Bro the Right Honourable Lord Farnham, Past Pro Grand Master, an event which has occasioned sorrow to every member of the Craft, it is ordered that Masonic Mourning shall consist of the printing of an 'In Memoriam' notice on the first summons issued for a meeting of each Lodge under the Grand Lodge following the date of this letter; and that the members of each Lodge shall stand in memory of Bro Lord Farnham at its next meeting immediately after the Lodge has been opened and before any business is transacted (except for the reading of any dispensation required to regularise the holding of the meeting)."

As a final observation, which I mention only because as a mistake it seems to becoming increasingly common, is that if the heading to the box is intended to be the Latin for "In memory", it is "In memoriam" not "In memorium".

Minutes

Rule 144 requires every Lodge to keep minutes and lays the responsibility for this equally on the Master and the Secretary. The minutes are to be read at the following regular meeting "(unless an exact copy has been sent to each member of the Lodge with the summons to the meeting) and submitted for confirmation as a true record of fact". The minutes of the previous meeting are not to be read or put for confirmation at any emergency meeting,[3] so that if an emergency meeting has been held there will be two sets of minutes for confirmation at the next regular meeting. It will be seen from this that the reading of the minutes may be dispensed with only if an exact copy has been circulated, so that a summary of the minutes is not sufficient.

It is generally considered that there are two grounds only on which the minutes may be challenged: accuracy of record, and propriety of record. As an illustration, if a statement made by a member at the previous meeting has been inaccurately recorded, the minutes should be amended, but if the statement that he made was untrue but accurately recorded, it should stand in the minutes, which are intended to be a true record of what was said, not a record of the truth of what was said. Similarly, it may be *proper* to record, for example, that "Brother So-and-so spoke disparagingly of the recent letter sent by the Provincial Grand Secretary" rather than record his actual words.

---

3   Except in so far as any such minutes relate to or affect the validity of the business – Rule 139.

The Board of General Purposes, which is anxious to encourage Lodges to save time at meetings by circulating the minutes in advance, recently (March 2005) found it necessary to comment on the excessive detail, particularly in relation to the ceremonial work of the Lodge, that seemed to be creeping into the minutes, the function of which "is to provide the formal record of the business transacted at each meeting of a Lodge, rather than a detailed description of every aspect of the ceremonies and administrative business". It noted that such lengthy minutes seemed to be in many cases linked with the increasing use of word processors, and suggested that Lodge Secretaries should restrict the minutes, in so far as they relate to the ceremonies, to identifying the ceremony, the candidate and the particular Brethren undertaking the work (if that was not immediately obvious from the offices such Brethren hold).

It is perhaps at this point worth reminding Brethren that the Minute Book must contain a record of "the names of all members present at each meeting of the Lodge, and of all visiting Brethren with the names and numbers of their Lodges and their Masonic ranks". It is not sufficient merely to refer to the Lodge Signature Book (which, interestingly, is mentioned in the Book of Constitutions only in Rule 127, in relation to unattached Brethren). The Board as long ago as 1959 took the view that this requirement was met if loose attendance sheets, which were then becoming common (and are no less so now), were irremovably affixed to the minutes of the meeting to which they refer, provided that each sheet was initialled by the Master or Secretary. It stressed, however, it did not wish to encourage the use of loose sheets to the exclusion of Signature Books and that all the names recorded in the Signature Book should continue to be recorded in the minutes. Just as signature sheets must be permanently affixed to the Minute Book, so must sheets containing the typed or printed minutes be permanently so affixed and initialled by the Secretary or Master *before being submitted for confirmation* by the Lodge.

Multiple ceremonies

With fewer candidates coming into Freemasonry, multiple ceremonies and multiple candidates for ceremonies are, in general, becoming less common. Rule 168 limits to two the number of candidates upon whom a Lodge may confer any particular degree on the same day, unless a dispensation is granted. When such a dispensation is granted by the Grand Master, it includes the following express term for an initiation: "This Dispensation is granted on the condition that the degree shall not be conferred on more than two candidates at one and the same time, the whole of the Ceremony to be performed on each occasion except the Charge, which may be given to all together;" so that if there are three or four candidates the ceremony has to be gone through twice. Apollo University Lodge, No. 357, has for many years annually received a dispensation from the Provincial Grand Master for Oxfordshire to confer degrees on more than two candidates, without the inclusion of any such restriction, so that in that Lodge the initiation, passing or raising of four or more candidates simultaneously is commonplace. Isaac Newton University Lodge at Cambridge was until very recently the only other Lodge with a tradition of such multiple ceremonies, but with the introduction of the new "Universities Scheme", which aims at "marrying up" universities with a Lodge in their vicinity, more Lodges can be expected in the future to adopt the practice.

While Rule 168 places a limit on the number of candidates for any one degree at a meeting, there is no restriction on the number of different degrees that may be worked, so that, at least in theory, it is possible for a Lodge to work all three degrees and the Installation in the course of a single meeting. If such a course is adopted, it is only considerate (and sensible) to take the degrees in descending order, so that Entered Apprentices and Fellow Crafts can time their arrival for the expected start of the ceremony or ceremonies they are permitted to attend. In these days when Lodges are being encouraged to have an experienced Brother accompany those Brethren when they retire while the second or third degree is worked, the practice of working the degrees in descending order, which was always a sound plan, has acquired even greater importance.

Taking in work

It has always been the case that some Lodges have so many candidates that they are overburdened with work, while others have a dearth and are crying out for work. The terms on which those in the former category are allowed to lay off some of their work with those in the latter are set out in Rule 173. The procedure is remarkably simple and informal, though the Rule is couched slightly off-puttingly in a negative way. If both Lodges concerned are under the United Grand Lodge of England, all that is required is a *written* request from one to the other, *signed* by the Master and Secretary of the requesting Lodge; it does not even have to be sent via the Grand Secretary or the Provincial or District Grand Secretary.[4]

---

4 In this context, as in some others, a communication sent by e-mail is not a sufficient compliance with the Rule.

When the ceremony has been carried out, the fact must be certified to the requesting Lodge and the Grand Secretary. Even if the two Lodges concerned are under different Grand Lodges, the only additional formality is that the request must be transmitted via the respective Grand Secretaries, with the Grand Secretary responsible for the requesting Lodge countersigning the request.

The reason for using Rule 173 need not be a redistribution of work between Lodges; most requests involving another Grand Lodge are because of the temporary relocation of the candidate so that it makes sense for him to be advanced to a higher degree in a Lodge more conveniently situated than his own mother Lodge.

Two points need to be specially noted in relation to the Rule. First, it may only be used to carry out a passing or a raising; a Lodge cannot *initiate* a candidate on behalf of another Lodge. Secondly, the Secretary of the requesting Lodge needs to keep a careful eye on the calendar; degrees conferred by request are a common reason for breaches of the twenty-eight-day period between degrees prescribed by Rule 172 (see Chapter 9).

Demonstrations

As has just been noted, Lodges from time to time have no candidates. They therefore sometimes fall back on a demonstration of another ritual or a rehearsal of the Lodge's usual ritual. Though superficially similar, the two are in essence quite different. A rehearsal by the Master and his Officers requires no special measures, and the Lodge need not even be Called Off while it is carried out, though it is better if it is, as that simple act marks the fact that the Lodge is not working a live ceremony. If, however, a Lodge wishes to allow a Master Mason (perhaps the Senior Warden, in anticipation of the work he may be called on to perform during his year as Master) to occupy the Chair for the rehearsal, it is essential that the Lodge be Called Off. (This is the logical conclusion from Rule 105(c) and Rule 119(b).)

On the other hand, a demonstration of the ritual of a recognised Grand Lodge (for which the arrangements should be made through the Grand Secretary's Office) may only be given if the following conditions are satisfied:

(a) only Master Masons are present at the demonstration;
(b) the Lodge has been closed, or is Called Off for the duration of the demonstration; and
(c) the Lodge room remains fully tyled throughout.

If the ritual is in a language other than English the *express permission* of the Board of General Purposes is required in addition. (It should also be noted that *no* demonstration of the ritual of another Grand Lodge may in any circumstances be given in a Lodge of Instruction.) The same conditions apply equally to reconstructions of historical forms of Craft ritual.

Two further points need to be noted. First, a demonstration is just that: there can be no question of a Lodge of another Constitution being permitted to confer a degree in a Lodge of the English Constitution or to meet in any territory over which the United Grand Lodge of England has exclusive jurisdiction (and, correspondingly, no dispensation may be granted for an English Constitution Lodge to hold a meeting or confer a degree within the territory of another Grand Lodge). Secondly, a demonstration of the extended Inner Working of the Board of Installed Masters must be accompanied by the same declaration as at a genuine Installation where the extended working is used (see below).

Calling Off and Calling On

If a Lodge is to work more than one ceremony in the course of a meeting, there are excellent reasons – practical as well as Masonic – for making a short break in the proceedings at one or more appropriate point. It is wrong in principle to interrupt a ceremony for the purpose, but there can be no objection to Calling Off the Lodge at a natural break point, and Calling On the Lodge when work is to be resumed. It is, however, essential that there should be a formal Call Off and Call On.

The other side of this particular coin – far more objectionable than a Call Off – is the practice in a few Lodges of taking administrative business (generally on a plea that time will be saved thereby) while the candidate has retired to restore himself. Even if he has only just been initiated and has still to receive the Charge, he is a member of the Lodge paying – or about to pay – a full subscription, and is entitled to participate in its business.

Different faiths

Under the United Grand Lodge of England, as under the Grand Lodges of Ireland and Scotland, the Volume of the Sacred Law is the Bible and it is always open while the Lodge is open (*Aims and Relationships of the Craft*, paragraph 4). Every candidate must normally take his obligations on the Bible or whichever Holy Book, according to his religion, imparts sanctity to an obligation taken on it. In the multicultural society in which we live, it is becoming much more common in

England and Wales for candidates not to be of the Christian faith, but it is actually nothing new in English Constitution Masonry. For example, Rudyard Kipling wrote in *Barrack Room Ballads – The Mother Lodge*:

> We'd Bola Nath, Accountant,
>   An' Saul the Aden Jew,
> An' Din Mohammed, draughtsman
>   Of the Survey Office too;
> There was Babu Chuckerbutty,
>   An' Amir Singh the Sikh,
> An' Castro from the fittin'-sheds,
>   The Roman Catholick!

A Lodge that has, or is in the process of acquiring, a tradition of taking candidates of differing faiths will probably need guidance only on the precise book on which an individual candidate will need to be obligated. But to a Lodge which has no such tradition the prospect may be a daunting one. The paramount consideration is that the candidate should be obligated on the Volume which is held by his particular creed to impart sanctity to an oath or promise taken upon it. The best source of information in any but the most obvious cases is almost certainly the candidate himself, and not only etiquette but also common sense dictates that he should be fully consulted not only on the identity of the Sacred Volume but also on the manner in which the obligation is to be taken on it (*e.g.* whether the Sacred Volume should be opened, whether he should kneel, or whether the obligation may be sealed by saluting the Sacred Volume). Indeed, he will probably himself produce the appropriate Sacred Volume for use in the ceremony. Such consultation should take place well before the day of the ceremony so that those Brethren who need to know may be adequately briefed. Some sensitivity may be called for here, and heavy-handedness on the part of the Master or the Director of Ceremonies is not only uncalled-for but likely to be counter-productive. The candidate's Sacred Volume must, of course, be treated with the appropriate reverence and respect.

The best practice is to place the Sacred Volume that is to be used to the west of the Bible, on the Master's pedestal if there is room, but if necessary on a small table immediately in front of the pedestal (for which purpose the kneeling-stool would be moved a few inches to the west). There is no compelling Masonic reason why that Sacred Volume should, if it has been opened, remain open once the obligation has been taken and (if appropriate in the particular case) sealed, but equally there is no reason why it should not, and, unless there is good reason according to the candidate's particular faith for so doing, closing it curtly at the end of the obligation may be seen as cavalier or even offensive.

Members of the Religious Society of Friends, or "Quakers" as they are more commonly known, are generally averse to taking any oath or obligation on the Bible, and instead make an affirmation. Accordingly the wording of the obligations is varied by substituting at the beginning: "I ...., being one of the people called Quakers, in the presence of this worthy [etc] Lodge .... do hereby seriously promise and declare that ...." and at the end: "These several points I do, as a Quaker, seriously declare and affirm that I will keep and observe......." As the candidate's affirmation is binding on him according to his faith, he does not seal it.

The extended Inner Working of the Board of Installed Masters

In 1926, the Board of General Purposes recommended to the Grand Lodge that the use of the extended Inner Working of the Board of Installed Masters by the relatively small number of Lodges which used it should cease. The move was strongly opposed by those Lodges that would have been affected, and as a result the following resolution was passed by the Grand Lodge in December 1926, which continues to regulate the use and demonstration of the extended Inner Working:

> "Grand Lodge takes note of the exceptional and traditional circumstances attaching in certain Lodges to the ceremonial Opening and Closing *in extenso* of a Board of Installed Masters. While it still deprecates the use of any signs, tokens, or words unknown to, or unrecognised by, the majority of English Installed Masters, it declares, in view of these circumstances, that, provided that there shall be incorporated in such ceremony a precise declaration by the Installing Master to the Master Elect that the signs, tokens, and words given in the course of the extended portion of the working are not essential to the Installation of a Master, and are not known to, or to be required from, Installed Masters generally, and that no further Degree in Masonry is being conferred, Lodges are permitted to perform the ceremony."

General powers of the Master

Even a perfunctory reading of the section of the Book of Constitutions dealing with Private Lodges shows that the Master of a Lodge has very extensive powers. It is equally clear that custom and practice place considerable restraints on the exercise of such powers, and it would be a brave Master who attempted to exercise more than a small fraction of them other than in exceptional circumstances. Such Brethren, however, do exist – and are generally the despair not only of their own Lodges but of the Metropolitan, Provincial or District authorities also.

For example, Rule 104(e) provides "No Brother has any right to claim advancement. The appointment of all Officers, except the Master, the Treasurer, and (if elected) the Tyler, is in the sole discretion and power of the Master." This (which was probably intended originally to silence both ambitious Brethren and the proponents of "Buggins' turn") certainly licenses the Master Elect to select his Officers with an unfettered hand, but it will not of itself protect him from the long-term consequences of taking too independent a line. The Master also has the power to lay a complaint against any of his Officers before the Lodge and with approval of a majority of the members present to displace him and appoint another in his place (Rule 120), but he should remember that any such resolution (which is hardly ever used in practice) may cause deep divisions in his Lodge. He also has a useful power in relation to certain visitors under Rule 126, which will be dealt with in the next chapter.

The Master may direct the alternative day (not more than seven days either way) on which a meeting which would otherwise fall on a prohibited day or a public holiday is to be held (Rule 139) and, by implication, he may also direct that the meeting is to be held on the regular day if the latter is merely a public holiday; he may also summon an emergency meeting, provided a dispensation has been obtained (Rule 140). He is *ex officio* a member of every committee of the Lodge and has the right to preside. He has an implied power to take the sense of a meeting without actually taking a vote (unless it should be requested) for the purpose of regulating the procedure in the Lodge as provided in Rule 155. He has a casting vote in the event of the votes on a matter being equal. He may allow (or refuse to allow) the fast track procedure for initiation permitted by Rule 160 (see Chapter 3). He may, in conjunction with the Secretary, request another Lodge to pass or raise a candidate for his Lodge (Rule 173). He may admonish a Brother for misbehaving in Lodge (Rule 180).

General duties of the Master

With powers there generally go duties, on the general principle that much is expected of those to whom much is given. The Master is reminded of many of these when he is first installed in the Chair of a Lodge by the Secretary reading the summary of the Antient Charges prior to his Obligation, but the Book of Constitutions also imposes duties. Of these, one of the most important laid upon him is contained in Rule 114: "The Master is responsible for the due observance of the laws by the Lodge over which he presides." Much can be summed up merely under this particular Rule, but there are many specific duties as well. The Master has, as we have already seen, the duty of keeping the Warrant of the Lodge safe and producing it at every meeting. He has the duty of satisfying himself in the case of a visitor from another Constitution that such Constitution is recognised by the Grand Lodge (Rule 125). He, together with his Wardens, holds the Lodge's property (other than that vested in special Trustees) on trust for the members of the Lodge (Rule 143), and has the responsibility, shared with the Secretary, of keeping minutes of Lodge meetings (Rule 144). He must certify that any candidate for initiation or joining is, in his opinion or that of the Lodge's committee, a suitable person to become a member of the Lodge – Rule 164(a). He must notify the Metropolitan, Provincial or District Grand Secretary, the Grand Inspector or the Grand Secretary, as the case may be, of any serious conviction – as defined by Rule 179A(a) – of any of the Lodge's members of which he is aware, whether or not the Brother concerned has reported the matter to him himself, as well as any case which is likely to bring Freemasonry into disrepute – Rule 179A(b) and (d).

Powers and duties of a Brother acting in the place of the Master

If the Master, though not occupying the Chair, is present, he is not deprived of his powers or absolved from the discharge of his duties (though if he has been temporarily displaced in accordance with the provisions of Rule 122, it is difficult to see how he could be held responsible or even criticised for any act or omission on the part of the Brother presiding). If he is absent, however, Rule 3 of the Book of Constitutions covers the situation: "Every Brother who shall, in accordance with the laws and procedure of Masonry, preside or act in ... any private Lodge ... for, or in the place of, any Officer or Brother who may be absent, shall, while so presiding or acting, have all the rights, powers, and duties of the Officer or Brother whose substitute he shall be or in whose place he shall act; he shall enforce all rules and regulations, and his acts shall have the same validity in all respects as those of such Officer or Brother, unless the contrary is expressly provided for in these laws and regulations." For this purpose it is immaterial whether the Brother presides because of the provisions of Rule 119(b) or because the Master has requested him to do so under Rule 119(d) or otherwise.

If the Master has died, resigned, moved away, or is otherwise prevented from discharging his office, the power and duty of summoning the Lodge (and by implication all other *necessary* powers and duties) devolve in accordance with Rule 119(a). A Senior Warden finding himself in this position by the operation of the Rule may well find himself also under pressure to act in accordance with the directions of more senior Brethren in the Lodge. Neither he nor they, however, should forget that the responsibility for what is done or not done in these circumstances rests with him – just as it will do in less than a year's time if he becomes Master in his own right.

Alms

Whether alms are collected during the meeting or afterwards at dinner, it is important that a clear statement should be made as to the object to which the collection is to be devoted. The Grand Secretary, as recently as February 2009, circulated to Lodges a paper giving guidance, which had been approved by specialist counsel, on the Charities Acts (the most recent being the Charities Act 2006) and the way in which they affect Lodges and individual Brethren. The relevant section reads:

"Use of charity money

"Where a fund is a charity, it can be used only for charity purposes – and only for those specified in the governing document. Money can be given to other charities with suitable purposes: it does not have to be spent directly on relieving poverty and so on. Registered charities are listed on the Charity Commission's website.

"Providing 'Christmas boxes' for the widows of deceased Brethren (unless the particular widow is truly in need) or flowers at funerals, though in the best Masonic tradition, are not charity purposes in law. They must not be paid for out of any charity fund. But such expenditure can be met out of the general funds of a Lodge or out of a non-charity fund or from collections (*e.g.* at table) which are not designated for a charity fund.

"Because of the restrictions placed on the use of charitable funds it is important that Lodges clearly identify the use to which the proceeds of any collection are intended to be put (just as when a raffle is held, the object to which the proceeds are to be applied must be clearly stated before any tickets are sold). Thus it will usually be the responsibility of the Master, if a collection is taken in Lodge, or perhaps the Almoner or Charity Steward if a collection is taken during or after the dinner, to make a clear announcement that the proceeds are to go to a named charity, or to the Lodge's charity fund, or to provide Christmas gifts to widows, or to a Lodge fund which is to be used for purposes that are benevolent, but not in law charitable. It is important that such funds are kept separate and distinct."

The Risings

The Risings are the established method of bringing before the Lodge any business that is not covered by the agenda printed on the summons. The words "Any Other Business" are the traditional way of showing the Risings on the summons. As Rule 140 forbids the transaction at an emergency meeting of any business not mentioned on the summons, it follows that there can be no Risings at an emergency meeting, neither may the words "Any Other Business" appear on the summons. Conversely at a regular meeting that common exchange between the Master and the Secretary – "Bro. Secretary, is there any other business?" – "Nothing before the Risings, Worshipful Master", or "Bro. Secretary, is there any other business before the Risings?" – "Nothing, Worshipful Master" – is strictly unnecessary even if the answer from the Secretary is in the affirmative!

The precise matters dealt with under each of the Risings vary from place to place, but in outline, the first Rising is generally devoted to communications from "Grand Lodge" (more properly from the Grand Secretary), the second Rising to communications from "Metropolitan, Provincial or District Grand Lodge", and the third to any remaining matters: notices of motion, propositions for initiation and joining, apologies, etc. Although the practice is unusual in and around London, it is common in many Provinces for visitors to convey greetings from their respective Lodges on the third Rising. This is a matter for individual Lodge practice, but purists would hold that unless a Brother has been specifically authorised, none but the Master has the right to convey such greetings.

Standing to order

In the course of the administrative business of a Lodge, Brethren will need to address the Master, and even if a Brother is in fact addressing the whole Lodge, he should always start by saluting and addressing the Master. If he has only a few words to say, it is entirely appropriate that he should hold the sign throughout. All too often, however, an inexperienced Brother will continue to stand to order for several sentences, only discharging the sign at the end of his remarks. A newly appointed Secretary is often the worst offender in this respect. As a general rule, if a Brother has more than a single sentence to say, he should salute the Master at the beginning and end of his remarks and stand naturally while he delivers himself of everything in between.

Closing in full

Many Lodges never close the Lodge formally in any but the first degree, merely resuming downwards if the ceremony has involved opening in the second or third. A few Lodges make a practice of always closing the Lodge in full in each degree in which it has been opened; others close in full in the degree in which they have just worked a ceremony so that the candidate may have the opportunity of seeing it on the occasion of his being passed or raised, as the case may be. What practice is adopted is a matter for each individual Lodge, which will doubtless have its own tradition in the matter. A purist would probably insist that closing in full is the only correct course, and he might well be right. The practice of resuming is, however, so widespread as to have become the norm, and if it has ever attracted the formal censure of Masonic authority, it is very many years since it did so.

"White tables"

For a good many years some Lodges have from time to time invited ladies and other non-Masons to join them at dinner, at a so-called "white table". More recently it has become increasingly common to invite them on such an occasion into the Lodge room after the Lodge has been closed or Called Off and give them a short talk or presentation on Freemasonry. There is little more that needs to be said about this practice, beyond observing, first, that it is greatly preferable that the Lodge should be closed rather than Called Off, so that the Brethren can accompany their guests out of the Lodge Room to the reception and dinner; and, secondly, that the Metropolitan, Provincial or District authorities should be made aware of what is to happen so that any necessary permission or dispensation for the wearing of regalia may be given. Occasionally, however, a Lodge asks whether it is permissible to invite non-Masons in while the Lodge is open and conduct some of the ritual work or Lodge business in front of them. In brief, the answer is "No". In a Private Lodge no non-Mason may be present while the Lodge is open; *no part* of the ceremonies of Initiation, Passing, Raising or Installation may be conducted with non-Masons present, since those ceremonies, to be valid, must take place in open Lodge; and the administrative business of a Lodge, besides being of a private nature, to be validly transacted must also be conducted in open Lodge. Similarly the Masonic ceremonial which accompanies a Private Lodge's Centenary or Bi-Centenary celebrations including the presentation of a Warrant, being "an official ceremony, the essential elements of which have been laid down by central Masonic authority" *must* be conducted while the Lodge is open and therefore with only Masons present.

There are, however, other Masonic activities which can take place while a Lodge is Called Off or after it has been closed, where there is no need to adopt a mysterious or secretive attitude, the most notable in the case of a Private Lodge being the dedication of a Banner "where an impressive show of Masonic ceremonial (as opposed to ritual) can be given without in any way compromising Masonic principles. In such instances, an important test is whether the Lodge feels comfortable with such a display and, provided that the local Masonic authority has no objection either generally or in relation to a particular activity, the Board considers that Lodges should not be discouraged from (or, conversely, pressed into) admitting their ladies and friends on such occasions. No Masonic signs **whatever** may be given on such occasions, as the Lodge is not open" (see *Information for the Guidance of Members of the Craft*: "Business Conducted with non-Masons Present").[5]

---

5 While Metropolitan, Provincial or District Grand Lodges may not carry out administrative Masonic business while non-Masons are present, they are not discouraged from admitting non-Masons to investitures, "which do not of themselves involve anything that an outsider may not see and are ... conducted by or on behalf of a recognised Masonic authority".

7

VISITING

You promise that no Visitor shall be received into your Lodge without due examination, and producing proper Vouchers of his having been initiated in a regular Lodge.

Number 15 of the Summary of the Antient Charges

"Visitors are the life-blood of Freemasonry" or "Visiting is what Freemasonry is all about". How often have we heard these sentiments – often expressed in those very words – when the toast to the visitors is proposed or replied to after dinner? Both statements can only be described as hyperbole, but the fact that they are made is a clear indication of how much a part of Freemasonry visiting is. Our Lodges could certainly carry on their work if they never saw a visitor from one year end to the next, but how much the poorer they would be as a result!

There is perhaps no area of Masonic activity in which etiquette is of greater importance than visiting, and like so much of Masonic etiquette, generally it comes down to what is good manners irrespective of the Masonic context.

The Rules

Visitors can only be admitted to the Grand Lodge with the permission of the Grand Master, may only speak with leave, and may not vote (Rule 10).

Rule 122 confers on the Rulers of the Craft the right to preside in any Lodge that they visit, and within their respective Metropolitan Area, Province, District or Group local Rulers enjoy a similar power. A little-used provision of the same Rule allows a Ruler of the Craft to authorise by commission a present Grand Officer of not less than Very Worshipful rank to preside in his stead at a specified meeting of a named Lodge not falling within a Metropolitan Area, Province or District.

Rule 123 allows the Grand Master to send any Grand Officer (present or past) to visit any Lodge, and Rule 124 confers broadly similar powers on Metropolitan,

Provincial and District Grand Masters. In such cases, the Brother sent to visit is to be placed on the immediate right of the Brother presiding.

A Brother of this Constitution must not be admitted as a visitor in a Private Lodge unless he is personally known to, and vouched for, by one of the Brethren present, or must "be well vouched for after due examination". If required, he must produce his Grand Lodge Certificate "and proof of good standing in his Lodge or Lodges" (Rule 125). The test laid down by the Rule is even more rigorous in the case of a visitor from another Constitution, who must not only produce his appropriate Grand Lodge Certificate and proof of good standing but must acknowledge that a belief in T.G.A.O.T.U. "is an essential Landmark of the Order"; and the responsibility for making sure that the other Constitution is one recognised by the United Grand Lodge of England is laid firmly on the Master. Finally, it is made explicit that a visitor is bound by any relevant by-laws of the Lodge he attends. It is worth noting, first, that a visitor does not have to be personally known to one of the members; it is sufficient if he is personally known to another visitor who does satisfy that test. Secondly, many Lodges are less diligent than they should be in checking the *bona fides*, and in particular the good standing, of visitors than the Rule requires.

Under Rule 126, the Master has power "to refuse admission to any visitor of known bad character or whose presence is in his opinion likely to disturb the harmony of the Lodge". This confers a sweeping power on the Master and will be examined in greater detail below.

We have already seen in Chapter 3 the disadvantages that an unattached Brother, particularly one who has become so by being excluded from the last Lodge of which he was a subscribing member, is subject to in the matter of visiting through the operation of Rule 127.

"So far the poet..."[1]

The protocol

Unless there are quite exceptional reasons, the only visitors admitted to the Grand Lodge are the most senior Brethren of recognised Grand Lodges and (though they attend far less often) the United Grand Lodge of England's representatives near such Grand Lodges. Such Brethren are normally seated in order of seniority of

---

1 See Preface.

their respective Grand Lodges, to the left of the Throne, behind the Grand Chaplain and any past Rulers who may be present. In the event that the number of such visitors is unduly large, the number on the dais is restricted to two, or even one, per Grand Lodge, with the "overflow" being accommodated in the same order of seniority in the second or third row of seats to the east of the Junior Grand Warden.

When a Ruler of the Craft visits a Private Lodge, "Grand Lodge rules" apply from the point when he or his accompanying Director of Ceremonies is announced until he retires from the dinner. Occasionally a Ruler pays a very informal visit indeed, as the purely personal guest of one of the members who is well known to him, and then the protocol may be truncated or even dispensed with – but such occasions are rare. On a normal visit, the Ruler's Director of Ceremonies, having been admitted, announces that, for example, the MW Pro Grand Master, Peter Geoffrey Lowndes, accompanied by a deputation of Grand Officers, is without and demands admission. (The person who is entitled to preside in the Lodge under Rule 122, which is so structured that at any given moment there is only one such person, *demands* admission; a past Ruler of the Craft, who is no longer entitled to demand admission, has in recent years *desired* admission; all others paying an official visit *request* admission.) Having been directed by the Master to admit him, his Director of Ceremonies calls out the Lodge's Director of Ceremonies and Assistant Director of Ceremonies and the two Deacons and they then process out of the door of the Lodge where the Ruler, together with his escort will be waiting. The escort consists of all those present who are Grand Officers of the year (other than subscribing members of the Lodge, who, however senior, are *never* included in an escort because they are *hosts*) and usually at least the more senior of the past Grand Officers who are visitors. (It should be noted, first, that Honorary Members of a Lodge are not excluded from the escort, and, secondly, that if one past Grand Officer of a particular rank is included then all the past Grand Officer of that rank must be included.) The procession enters the Lodge in ascending order of seniority, with the Brethren called to order by the Lodge's Director of Ceremonies, who leads the right-hand file. It opens out into a double column, halts when the leading Brethren are a few paces short of the dais, and turns inwards while the Ruler passes through to the Master's pedestal where he is offered the gavel. Normally the gavel will be declined, but if the Ruler is attending in order to carry out a ceremony of Installation, it will be accepted and he will assume the Chair. The procession is then "rolled up" from the rear and, after the Grand Officers and others in it have moved to their places, the Ruler is saluted.[2]

A past Ruler or other very senior Grand Officer standing in for a Ruler at a major function such as a Lodge Bi-Centenary is received in the same manner (with the differences in the announcement already noted), except that he is not offered the gavel, since he is not entitled under Rule 122 to preside in the Lodge.

It is not currently the normal Grand Lodge practice for a Ruler to retire before the Lodge has been closed, but if for some reason it is found necessary for him to do so, his Director of Ceremonies will call out the Lodge's Director of Ceremonies, Assistant Director of Ceremonies and Deacons to lead the procession, place the Ruler centred immediately behind them, followed two by two in descending order of seniority by the Grand Officers who entered with him in procession earlier. If the Brethren have not already been called to order, they will be called on to stand while the Ruler retires.

Under normal circumstances, as soon as the Lodge has been closed the Ruler's Director of Ceremonies calls for the first verse of the National Anthem, which is followed by the closing hymn, under cover of which a procession is formed. This consists of the Director of Ceremonies, Assistant Director of Ceremonies and Deacons (seniors on the right) at the front, followed by the Master, behind the Junior Deacon, and the Ruler, on the Master's right, behind the Senior Deacon; thereafter the Wardens and the remaining Grand Officers who entered in procession with the Ruler fall in behind to complete the procession.

Just as a past Ruler or other very senior Grand Officer standing in for a Ruler at a major function is not offered the gavel, since he is not entitled under Rule 122 to preside in the Lodge, so he does not normally (but see below) take the place on the right of the Master in the outgoing procession; instead he has a place of honour in the *centre* (*i.e.* like the Master) but *behind* the Wardens.

The protocol is rendered more complex when (as happens much more frequently nowadays – and indeed is generally the case – since the formation of London into a Metropolitan Area) the Metropolitan, Provincial or District Grand Master (or his Deputy or Assistant) is also present. In such a case the local Ruler will first demand admission. After he has been admitted in accordance with the

---

2   The current Grand Lodge practice is that this is done before the Brethren resume their seats, but occasionally the former practice is followed and the Brethren are directed to sit, before being immediately called again to order for the salute.

protocol adopted locally, the Ruler (or substitute) will be admitted as set out above. The outgoing procession is varied by placing the Ruler *or substitute* on the Master's right and the local Ruler on the Master's left so that they are three abreast. If, as is the case in many Provinces, the Provincial sword and standards are carried when the Provincial Grand Master visits officially,[3] the Provincial Grand Sword Bearer is placed immediately in front of the Master (*not* the Provincial Grand Master) and the Provincial Grand Standard Bearers immediately behind the Master, one in front of each of the Wardens.

A single Grand Officer sent formally by the Grand Master to visit a Private Lodge is seated on the right of the Brother presiding (Rule 123) and therefore has precedence not only of any other Grand Officer who may be present but also of, for example, the Provincial Grand Master, his Deputy or Assistant (though generally matters are so arranged that any "conflict" either does not arise or, if it does, is entirely friendly in its nature). He will normally enter the Lodge before it is opened, but if for some reason his entry is delayed, he merely *requests* admission. In the outgoing procession he is placed behind the Senior Warden and is not centred. Although he may have displaced the Provincial Grand Master (or his Deputy or Assistant) from the seat on the Master's right, the former still retains his position on the Master's right in the outgoing procession (but the visiting Grand Officer does take precedence of all but the most senior Provincial Ruler present).

The Grand Lodge protocol is mirrored, with local variations, in Metropolitan Areas, Provinces and Districts. For example, in some Provinces a Provincial Grand Warden representing the Provincial Grand Master is accompanied by a Director of Ceremonies (not necessarily the Provincial Grand Director of Ceremonies, his Deputy or Assistant). In many, the Brethren forming an escort do not remain outside when the Lodge is opened, but are called out with the Director of Ceremonies, Assistant Director of Ceremonies and Deacons when the guest of honour is announced; in at least one Province the Lodge's Director of Ceremonies is responsible for organising both the escort and the outgoing procession, with the Provincial Director of Ceremonies being responsible merely for calling the

---

3   The Grand Lodge's sword and standards are not customarily carried when the Grand Master or another Ruler visits a Metropolitan, Provincial or District Grand Lodge or any Private Lodge. An apparent exception to this at the Inauguration in October 2003 of the Metropolitan Grand Lodge of London was, in truth, no exception, as on that occasion the *Grand Lodge* was opened "as a Metropolitan Grand Lodge" and subsequently formed into the Metropolitan Grand Lodge of London.

Brethren to order, as the guest of honour enters the Lodge, seeing him saluted and attending to any wine-taking or toast involving him at the after-proceedings.

The etiquette

Any Brother who visits a Lodge should be prepared to establish his *bona fides* as a Freemason, as required by Rule 125, though if he is introduced as a guest of one of the members he is unlikely to be called on to do so. If he is not likely to be known to any of the members, he will be well advised to have with him his Grand Lodge Certificate, as well as some evidence that he is in good standing with his Lodge; a clearance certificate would be a work of supererogation, but a recent summons to his Lodge showing him as a member or an Officer should be sufficient. Even so, he should not expect to be admitted on the basis of documentary evidence, but be prepared to undergo an examination in his knowledge of the signs, tokens and words of the degree or degrees in which the Lodge will be working. He should not regard such a test as an imposition not to be borne. I remember the case, a good many years ago, of a relatively junior Grand Officer who wished to visit a Lodge on the other side of the Atlantic and had prudently provided himself with a letter of introduction from the Grand Secretary, impressed with the seal of the Grand Lodge. When he was asked by the Lodge he was visiting to undergo a full examination he chose to take umbrage. On his return to England he complained to the then Grand Secretary, no doubt expecting that a serious complaint would be made to the other Grand Lodge concerned. To his chagrin he found that he was the one to be roundly rebuked for his attitude.

We have already noted that by virtue of Rule 125 a visitor is bound by any relevant by-laws of the Lodge he attends. This may even mean that in some cases, such as The Grand Stewards' Lodge (the by-laws of which prohibit the introduction of visitors except at the Installation Meeting), a visitor is even precluded from attending. Some Lodges as a matter of course, and others if there may be private or even contentious business to discuss, put on the summons an item "To receive visitors at ..... p.m.", and even if the practice may not be enshrined in the Lodge's by-laws, most would agree that a visitor should respect the Lodge's wishes.

There is, indeed, no general right for any Brother, other than one falling within the scope of Rules 122 to 124, to visit any Lodge he chooses. The Board of General Purposes has very recently (September 2007) found it necessary to give guidance on this matter:

"The Board has been asked to express an opinion as to whether any Brother who is in good standing in the Craft has an inalienable right to visit any Lodge that he may choose. From time to time Brethren cause embarrassment to a Lodge or to individual members of it by seeking to visit either by prior invitation or by arriving on the day of the meeting.

"The Board is aware that under some Constitutions the 'right of visitation' is regarded as a landmark, but has concluded that it enjoys no such status under this Constitution. In particular, it does not figure in either the document *Aims and Relationships of the Craft* (adopted by the United Grand Lodge of England in September 1949, in common with the Grand Lodge of Ireland and the Grand Lodge of Scotland) or in *Basic Principles for Grand Lodge Recognition*. The Board has concluded that the question is as much a matter of common sense and basic good manners as of Masonic principle, and hopes that the Grand Lodge will endorse the following statement.

"1. The custom of visiting has a long and honourable history in English Freemasonry and ought not to be discouraged. Brethren are, however, reminded that while every Freemason in good standing is *eligible* (subject to Rule 127 of the Book of Constitutions) to attend Lodges other than his own as a visitor, he is not necessarily *entitled* to do so.

"2. There are certain Brethren on whom Rules 122 to 124 confer the right to be present at a meeting, either in their own capacity or as the emissary of the Grand Master or a Metropolitan, Provincial or District Grand Master.

"3. For visitors in the ordinary course, admission to any Lodge is subject to the power of the Master (under Rule 126) to refuse admission to any visitor of known bad character or whose presence is *in his opinion* likely to disturb the harmony of the Lodge; and apart from the fact that some Lodges have in their by-laws a restriction on the admission of visitors, every Lodge is entitled to expect a visitor to be properly introduced by a member (or, where a Lodge has indicated its willingness to accept visitors, by a suitable Masonic authority such as a Metropolitan, Provincial or District Grand Secretary).

"4. The Board deprecates any deliberate solicitation of an invitation to attend a Lodge by someone who can claim no more than acquaintance with the Brother whom he wishes to adopt as his host, but whom the making of the approach may place in an embarrassing position.

"5. Paragraphs 3 and 4 apply equally to the meal which follows, or occasionally precedes, a meeting of a Lodge."

Although the statement was very carefully worded, it was clear even before the Grand Lodge met to consider the Board's Report that it had been misinterpreted, and the President therefore, in introducing the Report, found it appropriate to add this clarification:

"The Board has been careful not to say that a visitor *must* only be introduced by a member of the Lodge; only that a Lodge is *entitled* to expect a visitor to be so introduced. A Lodge is always free to waive its entitlement in this respect if it so desires. So that, for example, a Brother who is temporarily staying in a particular area may perfectly properly make contact with the Secretary of a Lodge in the vicinity to find out whether it will be in order for him to attend as a visitor, and in many, if not most cases, he will be made very welcome. What such a Brother must not do, however, is insist that he has a right to visit the Lodge and try to force himself upon it. Moreover he should not expect automatically to be invited to the after-proceedings and, if he is, should at least offer to pay the cost of his dinner."

The Board's Report expressly mentioned the Master's power under Rule 126 "to refuse admission to any visitor of known bad character or whose presence is in his opinion likely to disturb the harmony of the Lodge." This sweeping power may be exercised if either of two tests, one objective, the other subjective, is satisfied. The objective test – known bad character – is unlikely to prove a cause of difficulty, but the subjective test can give rise to problems. Although it turns on the opinion of the Master, the Master must have grounds for his opinion and the reason why the Lodge's harmony might be disturbed must not be a trivial or unreasonable one, *e.g.* the colour of the visitor's hair. The Rule, in effect, picks up the words addressed by the Master to every new initiate: "... you are never to put on that badge should you be about to visit a Lodge in which there is a Brother with whom you are at variance or against whom you entertain animosity". It also provides a similar protection to members as the ability to veto a candidate for initiation or joining by use of a black ball: the harmony and enjoyment of the existing members of a Lodge is paramount. Whilst at first sight this may make the decision for the Master an easy one, the reality may be a very different matter, and the Master may be called on to exercise great wisdom and not a little tact. The fact is that refusing admission to a visitor may cause as much disharmony in a Lodge as allowing him admission. Unless he is trying to force himself on the Lodge without an invitation, a visitor is likely to have a host who has invited him and with whom the Master will have to contend: "But I've paid for his dinner, and anyway he's driven forty miles to accept *my invitation*; you can't just send him away like this!" Well, the Master can – and probably should if he has substantial reason to believe that the confrontation has been deliberately contrived. But it takes a courageous Master to do that – and a Master who is sure of his ground and, perhaps, confident that his future career in Masonry is not going to be blighted (or who is wholly unconcerned at the thought). Perhaps someone will talk high-mindedly of the duties of hospitality towards a guest. An incident such as this, which may lead to, or be the result of, a trial of strength between two Brethren or even factions within a Lodge, is fortunately very rare, but its occurrence is not confined to the colourful imagination of an Assistant Grand Secretary casting around for a graphic example to illustrate a point. The Master will probably decide that discretion is the better part of valour, and choose to call the bluff of the objector rather than be accused of being *inhospitable*.

The duties of hospitality are often invoked, but they do not exist on one side alone: a host certainly has a duty to his guest, but a guest also has a duty to his host. If you visit me in my home, as a good host I would offer you refreshment, but I have the right to expect that you will not repay my hospitality by deliberately pouring the cup of coffee that I give you over my carpet. Much of what follows in this chapter is an illustration of this simple point.

A visitor should endeavour in most respects to conform to the custom of the Lodge he visits. For example, he should endeavour to comply with its dress code (see Chapter 1). As another example, the practice of visitors giving greetings on the third Rising is by no means universal, and a Lodge may not welcome a visitor choosing to so do in defiance of the Lodge's own custom. This principle, however, has its limits and a visitor will be behaving perfectly properly if he stands to order during the obligation in the same manner, and discharges the sign at the same time, as he would in his mother Lodge. Indeed there is a risk in trying to follow too closely the minutiae of an unfamiliar ritual, that he will merely make himself look inept; far better to stick boldly to what he is used to. If he subsequently becomes a joining member of the Lodge, then he must adopt its ritual and practices, but as a visitor he may (and generally should) quite properly adhere to what he knows.

By the same token a visitor, unless he has been specifically asked to prompt, should almost invariably refrain from prompting during a ceremony: a prompt is not only "bad form", it may also be unnecessary, or inappropriate to the Working used by the Lodge, and he should proceed on the assumption that the Master, Immediate Past Master or Director of Ceremonies has made a suitable arrangement within the Lodge for prompting. The only exception to this precept is when the Master or some other Officer completely dries up and no prompt is forthcoming from anyone in the Lodge; then and only then is a prompt permissible – but even then the prompter places himself at risk of being criticised.

Another instance where the custom of the Lodge will have a bearing arises in the ceremony of Installation. "It has in recent years become the almost universal practice not to include visiting Master Masons in the perambulations, either from a mistaken belief that the duties of hospitality render it discourteous to ask visitors to join in the salutes (though no such scruples extend to the Inner Working) or from a – perhaps well-founded – suspicion that they may not be equal to the task."[4] Properly all Master Masons, Fellow Crafts and Entered Apprentices should take part in the perambulations and the salutes, but in a well-attended meeting it may be impracticable for all of them to do so, and therefore it is natural that visiting Master Masons should be asked to resume their seats while only the members of the Lodge participate in this part of the ceremony. As a matter of etiquette, a visitor should neither object to joining the perambulations if it is the custom of the Lodge, nor thrust himself forward if it is not.

Lodge Representatives

It is by no means uncommon for Lodges to form affiliations with other Lodges. Sometimes these are no more than a simple tie-up between two Lodges; sometimes it is a significant grouping with a structure of its own, such as the Public School Lodges' Council, the Federation of School Lodges or the Circuit of Service Lodges. Some quite old Lodges still have a by-law by which the Masters of the other Lodges in the grouping (almost invariably named in it) are to be

---

4 *Emulation Working Today* – Lewis Masonic, 2007

Honorary Members of the Lodge during their year as Master. Such a by-law will not now be permitted, and therefore often the by-laws nowadays contain a note to the effect that the Masters of those other Lodges shall be "honoured guests" during their year, or the Lodge passes a resolution each year to a similar effect. In yet other cases it is merely the custom to invite the Master once, say, a year (and in many Provinces it is not uncommon for such a reciprocal arrangement to exist between Lodges meeting in the same town). Such Brethren, though they may be accorded special privileges because of their representative capacity, are visitors like any other and subject to the same Rules and considerations of etiquette.

Lodge visits

Sometimes the link between Lodges goes further than regular invitations to the respective Masters; the Master and Officers, with other members, pay a collective visit and may even work a ceremony for the host Lodge. A similar arrangement on a "one-off" basis is also not uncommon. When such a visit takes place the Master and Officers of the visiting Lodge may wear neither their own collars, nor those of the Officers of the host Lodge (see Chapter 2). It is, however, also possible to have a variation on this, so that the host Lodge is either closed or Called Off temporarily, and the visiting Lodge then holds a meeting by dispensation under its own Warrant (in which case, of course, the Master and Officers may wear their collars – but the Master and Officers of the host Lodge must remove theirs).

General courtesies

It ought not to need saying, but almost all of us do neglect it from time to time, that a "bread and butter" letter should as a matter of course follow a visit. This is only a matter of good manners and the reciprocal obligations of hospitality, not specifically of Masonic etiquette. Sometimes a host will tell his guest not to bother to write (in more or less forcible terms!) but otherwise a guest ought to write to thank him. A hand-written letter is the most polite, since the writer will obviously have put himself to trouble in penning it. A typed (or word-processed) letter, however, is perfectly acceptable, and in this increasingly electronic age an e-mail may well soon become the norm. If a Brother is the guest of the Lodge, however, he should always write to the Secretary to thank the members for their hospitality. If a Lodge has paid a collective visit, the Master or Secretary should write on behalf of all.

A pleasing courtesy that is still widely observed is that when a Provincial Grand Master receives an invitation, that he is minded to accept, to visit a Lodge in London or another Province he will write to the Metropolitan or Provincial Grand

Master to tell him of the invitation and his intentions in regard to it. It is likely, but not a foregone conclusion, that he will be told not only that he is very welcome in accepting the invitation but also that he will be welcome to wear his chain (see also Chapter 2).

Disqualification from visiting

The subject of unattached Brethren has already been dealt with in Chapter 3. Nevertheless, it is worth elaborating on some of the points here, as Rule 127 is not as well understood as it should be by a great many Brethren, including some quite senior Freemasons. While he remains entitled to attend any Lodge of which he is an Honorary Member as often as he wishes, a Brother who has ceased to be a subscribing member of all his Lodges is placed under a serious disability as regards visiting. If, *but only if,* he became unattached as a result of being excluded from his last remaining Lodge under either Rule 148 or Rule 181, he may not attend *any* Lodge or Lodge of Instruction as a visitor unless and until he joins or rejoins a Lodge. If he became unattached as a result of resigning from his last remaining Lodge, even if he was indebted to it at the time, he remains free to visit any Lodge once, *and once only,* unless and until he joins or rejoins a Lodge, though he may attend Lodges of Instruction without any restriction. There is a popular misconception that such an unattached Brother may visit any Lodge once a year, but a misconception is exactly what it is. Once an unattached Brother has visited a Lodge, he must cross it permanently off his list of Lodges to visit.

Because these disabilities exist, it is the responsibility of the Master of a Lodge to make sure (and to take the blame himself in the event of a breach of the Rule) that unattached Brethren are admitted to his Lodge only if it has been ascertained that they are not precluded by Rule 127 from attending. But it should go without saying that it is even more the responsibility of a Brother's host to ensure that he does not introduce as a visitor a Brother who is not entitled to attend.

Unfortunately, apart from those who are ignorant of the provisions of the Rule, fail to understand them, or do not trouble to find out whether they apply, there are Brethren who are prepared to turn a blind eye to breaches of the Rule because they regard the Rule as silly or even unfair. It is suggested that there is nothing unfair or even silly about it. The Rule exists because what *is* unfair is that someone should be able to enjoy almost all the privileges of Masonry without paying so much as a penny for them. This should be self-evident in the case of those who have become unattached by their own voluntary act of resignation (though many still seem to benefit from the blind eye).

Rule 127 places a Brother who has become an Honorary Member of his only Lodge under the same disability as one who has chosen to abandon his Masonic career (or, at least, to place it "on hold"). Both the Grand Secretary and various Masonic publications regularly receive letters from Brethren suggesting that it is more or less an open scandal that a Brother who has been elected to Honorary Membership of his only Lodge should be debarred from attending any other Lodge more than once (and they seem in this context always to remember that it is *only once*) when Honorary Membership is meant to be a reward for his valued services. Well, he does have a reward: he has an unfettered right to attend the Lodge that has made him an Honorary Member (and if the subscription is a full dining one, he has the option of a number of free meals for life); that is entirely a matter for that Lodge. But no Lodge should have a right to give an individual a completely free run of the whole Craft. "But what harm would it do to change the Rule for Honorary Members?" they go on to ask. The answer, of course, is that one isolated case would have very little effect. Masons, however, are no different from other people: if they see a gap in the hedge, they will make for it, and if a sufficiently large number were to be given a "free ride" then Grand Lodge dues would have to go up for everybody else. A further consequence would be that Lodges (and their Brethren) that were sparing in awarding Honorary Membership would, in effect, be subsidising those that were more generous – not to say profligate.

To liken unattached Brethren who visit in breach of Rule 127 to those who travel on the railways without a ticket might be putting it too high, but there is a definite analogy between the two. Sometimes the fault will be one of ignorance, but a fault it is for all that, and ought not to be encouraged. Does it *really* matter? Only if you believe that Freemasonry is a serious organisation with a serious purpose. (So take that as a "Yes".).

8

BEHAVIOUR

To act on the Square, observe a proper deportment in the Lodge, pay due and becoming respect to the Worshipful Master and his presiding officers, to abstain from all political or religious disputes which might breed dissension among the Brethren, and in time entail a scandal on the Craft.

First Lecture, Section 7

This will not be a long chapter – not because behaviour in the Lodge is an unimportant subject, but because most of what needs to be said on the matter has already been dealt with in the earlier chapters of this book. As a general observation, however, where behaviour is concerned, regard should always be had to the established custom of the particular Lodge. Some Lodges do adopt a very formal style of behaviour; others are very much more relaxed. A member should conform to the practice of the Lodge he has joined, and a visitor should, as a matter of good manners, conform to the practice of the Lodge he is visiting. Neither should set out deliberately to behave with a lesser – or, for that matter, a greater[1] – degree of formality than is the particular Lodge's custom.

Two words would suffice to sum up the subject matter of this chapter: due decorum. Freemasonry is not a lark; organised English Freemasonry would not have survived for nearly three hundred years if that were all it was. It has a serious moral content, for all that it is convivial and enjoyable. Brethren should therefore behave with an appropriate degree of solemnity, and the following words from No. 6 of the Antient Charges – "*Of* BEHAVIOUR – 1. IN THE LODGE WHILE CONSTITUTED" – are as pertinent today as when they were originally framed:

---

1 There is a frightful tendency on the part of some Brethren to imagine that the more elaborate a procedure or form of words is, somehow the "better" it is. This is not so: pomposity should not be confused with politeness. See also the discussion below on the use of "Worshipful".

"You are not to hold private committees, or separate conversation, without leave from the master; nor to talk of anything impertinently or unseemly, nor interrupt the master or wardens, or any brother speaking to the master; nor behave yourself ludicrously or jestingly while the lodge is engaged in what is serious and solemn; nor use any unbecoming language upon any pretence whatsoever, but to pay due reverence to your master, wardens, and fellows, and put them to worship."

Absolutely taboo is the discussion of religion or politics. This is so deeply ingrained in English (and, of course, Irish and Scottish) Masonry as to be tantamount to a landmark.

In this increasingly electronic age the use of mobile telephones and other hand-held communication devices is becoming widespread. In March 2002 the Board of General Purposes reported to the Grand Lodge: "Brethren with mobile telephones are reminded that they should be switched off during Lodge meetings. If an urgent call is expected, arrangements should be made for it to be received by the Tyler." The main mischief at which the Board's Report was aimed was the intrusive ringing of mobile telephones, but the sending and receiving of text messages or e-mails during a meeting is equally a breach of proper manners. More than that, it detracts from the enjoyment of the Lodge meeting, not only of the neighbours of the owner of the telephone, but of the owner himself. One of the great pleasures of Freemasonry should be the fact that once the Inner Guard has closed the door of the Lodge Room, the outside world and its pressures are shut out for an hour or two. The newer generations of mobile telephones can also take photographs, another matter on which the Board has reported recently (September 2005):

"Brethren are reminded that whilst there is no objection to the taking of group photographs in a Lodge Room in connection with a special meeting, the taking of photographs during meetings (including any procession immediately before or after a meeting) is prohibited. The prohibition extends to any purported reconstruction after a Lodge has been closed of any part of the proceedings while the Lodge was open. Within Freemasons' Hall such group photographs may, subject to the permission of the Grand Secretary, be taken in a Lodge Room, but photographs in or of other parts of the building must not be taken unless special permission has been given by or on behalf of the Board of General Purposes."

It is a regrettable fact that at almost any large meeting (generally of the Grand Lodge or a Metropolitan, Provincial or District Grand Lodge) one or more Brethren feel the need to have a permanent photographic record of the occasion. Quite apart from the fact that any such photograph is taken in breach of the edict quoted above, flash photography (which is generally required because of the subdued lighting) is both distracting and discourteous. In most cases the breach is the result of ignorance, but there is no doubt that a minority of the Brethren who take photographs are well aware that they are flouting the edict in so doing – and are not deterred.

The Officers should arrive in good time for meetings, and come properly prepared to carry out the duties of their offices to the best of their ability. If an Officer knows that, for some reason, he will be unable to attend a meeting, it is only good manners (as well as a kindness to the Master, Director of Ceremonies and others) to make the fact known as soon as he is aware of it himself. Plenty of warning should also be given if an Officer knows that he will be late arriving; it is not fair to others that the start of a meeting is delayed because it is assumed that he will arrive at any moment, or that some other Brother is pressed into service at the last minute, without any opportunity to prepare himself. Every Brother ought, indeed, to make every effort to attend punctually at the time stated in the summons, rather than cause the Lodge's proceedings to be repeatedly interrupted by latecomers.

The Tyler should be expected to give a report only at a point when the Lodge's proceedings will not be unduly interrupted, and should therefore almost never break in upon a ceremony except when the candidate retires from, or is about to be readmitted to, the Lodge. Neither a member nor a visitor should make himself difficult to the Tyler without very good reason if the latter refuses to interrupt the ceremony with a report; equally the Tyler should not deliberately hold Brethren outside the door of the Lodge when there is no good reason for him to do so.

The procedure on the admission of a latecomer varies from Lodge to Lodge. In some Lodges the Director of Ceremonies will meet every Brother at the door, or collect him as soon as he has saluted and given his apologies; in others the Director of Ceremonies will only treat visitors (or only Brethren "in dark blue") in this way, leaving members of the Lodge to find their own way to their places. It is best that a Director of Ceremonies should err on the side of courtesy, but a visitor should not feel, or give the impression that he feels, he has been slighted if he is not escorted to a place by the Director of Ceremonies.

In addressing the Master, the correct formula is always "Worshipful Master"; "Master" is both disrespectful and wrong, even if the person using the formula is himself a Worshipful Brother. A Past Master may feel that, being a Worshipful Brother himself, he is entitled to dispense with the prefix in addressing the Master, but, quite apart from this reasoning being fallacious, if he does so he will set a bad example to more junior Brethren who being unaware of the alleged reasoning, let alone of the fact that it is misconceived, will be tempted to follow suit. Equally, "Very Worshipful Master" or "Right Worshipful Master", if the Master has a higher personal rank, is sycophantic and wrong. It is best to regard this as a matter of simple respect for the office (which is the highest a Lodge has in its power to confer on any of its members) and while the Lodge is open, whoever is in the Chair should be addressed by the indivisible title "Worshipful Master".

On a similar level, no other office has "Worshipful" as a part of its title, so that the usage "Worshipful Brother Secretary" or "Worshipful Brother Junior Warden" is, it is suggested, wrong as a matter of principle, since the prefix "Worshipful", except in the case of the Master, belongs to the *individual* and not to the *office*.

Whilst it cannot be said that to address or refer to someone as "Worshipful Brother Smith" is wrong, it is unnecessary, unless the Lodge is one that goes in for a great degree of formality. To refer to someone as "Worshipful" in the third person (*e.g.* "as Worshipful Brother Smith has just observed") is less stilted than to address him in such a way ("Worshipful Brother Smith, have you any observations to offer?"). Even less desirable, however, is the uneasy mixture of the formal and the informal, more commonly met with at dinner than in the Lodge, represented by the prefix "Worshipful" with a Brother's first name alone. "Brother Smith" is correct – and quite sufficient; "Worshipful Brother Smith" is acceptable, as in some circumstances is "Brother John"; but "Worshipful Brother John" is neither one thing nor the other and should be avoided.

Prompting in the course of a ceremony should be confined to those Brethren whose task it is according to the custom of the particular Lodge. In many Lodges it is the duty of the Immediate Past Master to act as prompter for the Master, and the Director of Ceremonies for all the other Officers, but custom varies greatly between Lodges. It is only a slightly less serious breach of etiquette for a member of the Lodge to give an unsolicited prompt than it is for a visitor to do so. It does nothing for the solemnity of a ceremony to have Brethren calling out prompts, even if a prompt is necessary (and the prompt given is accurate). It can be very demoralising for a Master or Officer to be interrupted in this way, and it does nothing to enhance the candidate's experience of the ceremony. Even for those whose job it is to prompt, it is important to know when to act to correct, and when to leave well alone – the latter being by far the more important. The Brother prompting must not only be able to recognise a mistake when it happens, he must also exercise an almost instantaneous judgement as to whether it is serious enough to be corrected, or whether (which is usually the case) it is relatively trivial and is much better left alone. He must also understand that he is a *prompter* and *not* a preceptor. The ceremony must be kept flowing with as little interruption as possible.

When the administrative business of the Lodge is being transacted or discussed, it should go without saying that all remarks should be addressed to or through the Worshipful Master, as the presiding Officer.

Finally, in some Lodges the National Anthem is sung after the Lodge has been closed, rather than before the first toast is drunk after dinner. If the anthem is sung, at whatever point, the Brethren should stand to attention during the singing. It is a regrettable fact that this particular observance, which was drummed into me when I was younger, is becoming noticeably less common, and that even Brethren who have a background in one of the Services frequently stand with their hands in front of them or behind their backs, rather than straight down at their sides with the thumbs to the front, when the National Anthem is sung.

9

PROBLEMS, PROBLEMS, PROBLEMS...

...there is scarcely a case of difficulty can occur in the Lodge in which that book will not set you right.

Ceremony of Installation

From time to time things go wrong. Sometimes it is the result of inaction or stupidity on someone's part, but most of the time mere chance is to blame. What is important is to ensure that, when a problem arises, things are not made worse by taking inappropriate action. Usually advice will be needed, and it is important that it should be sought from the right quarter. An expedient that was being increasingly resorted to some seven or eight years ago was posting an enquiry on the internet and waiting for the replies to come in. Such enquiries often brought forth a variety of different answers, and I am sorry to say that the correct answers did not always come from the Brethren with the highest ranks. The Board of General Purposes has firmly discouraged this practice as can be seen from the booklet *Information for the Guidance of Members of the Craft*[1]

"It has been brought to the notice of the Board that some Brethren are using the internet not only to make contact with other Freemasons, which may be unexceptionable, but also as a means of seeking guidance on questions which should properly be addressed to their Provincial or District Grand Secretaries, from whom authoritative answers are available. Such enquiries frequently elicit a variety of different answers (of which many are, in the nature of things, likely to be wrong) and the Board considers that directing questions on protocol and similar matters to those participating in an internet forum is inappropriate both for that reason and because of the nature of the subject-matter involved."

---

1 "Internet – Forums and 'Chat Rooms'"

Seeking advice from the Metropolitan, Provincial or District Grand Secretary is usually the prudent course, but it may first be sensible to consult the booklet *Information for the Guidance of Members of the Craft*, which is a veritable goldmine of information on matters where the Board of General Purposes has found it necessary to report to Grand Lodge.

Contingencies affecting the Master Elect

Most of the worst problems seem to centre on the death, incapacity or unavailability for one reason or another of the Master or the Master Elect. The Master Elect may die, suffer some disqualification, decide he does not wish to go into the Chair after all, or simply be temporarily unavailable on the day appointed for the Installation.

The last of these is usually the simplest to deal with. Given sufficient notice, the date of the Installation Meeting can be moved by dispensation under Rule 139(c) by not more than twenty-eight days in either direction, which will take care of most emergencies. If on the day of the Installation itself the Master Elect is unavoidably prevented from attending, the Installation is postponed and must take place within five weeks (if necessary, at an emergency meeting); if the Master Elect fails to attend on the second date, the outgoing Master continues in office for another year and invests the Officers (if any) chosen by the Master Elect. Any Brother installed or invested at the postponed Installation meeting is deemed for the purposes of Rule 9 and Rule 105 to have filled the office for a full year at the date of the next regular installation meeting.

If the Master Elect dies, becomes disqualified or incapacitated, or gives written notice to the outgoing Master that he does not intend to accept the Mastership, then another Brother must become Master in his stead. If the event takes place seven days or more before the date of the meeting, Rule 106 applies, and a summons, or further summons, is issued to all the members of the Lodge, stating what has happened and giving notice that a new Master is to be elected on the regular day of the Installation.[2] The Master then elected must be installed within five weeks, unless the outgoing Master is elected to continue in office, when no installation is necessary (or permissible) and he may proceed at once to appoint

---

2   By a proviso to the Rule, if there is not less than two months between the election and installation meetings and the event occurs not less than six weeks before the latter, an emergency meeting *may* be held to elect another Master.

and invest his Officers. If, however, the event takes place less than seven days before the installation meeting, Rule 107 applies and the outgoing Master continues in office, investing the Officers (if any) chosen by the Master Elect and appointing any others himself.

One other contingency may arise. A motion might be moved under Rule 105(b) that the Master Elect be not installed. Such an event is very unusual (and potentially very divisive), and the procedure is very cumbersome. To carry the motion a majority, on a ballot, of three-quarters of the members *present* is required, the largest majority provided for anywhere in the Book of Constitutions (other than on a ballot for membership). If it is carried, a new Master must forthwith be elected, to be installed within five weeks (with the usual provisions as to deemed service in office for a full year). Because of the divisive nature of such a motion, it is suggested that it should be used only in a really serious case – such as the Master Elect being suddenly convicted of, or charged with, a crime such as would have to be reported under Rule 179A (see below). It should not be trivialised by using it in the case of a disagreement over, say, his choice of Officers.

Contingencies affecting the Master

The Master of a Lodge *cannot resign from his office*. The only option available to him is to resign from the Lodge, thereby terminating his Mastership. If the Master dies or resigns from the Lodge, *another Master cannot be elected* to fill the vacancy. The same provisions apply, under Rule 119, as if he were "removed" (which is a use of the word in its older, and now secondary, meaning of moving away[3]) or prevented by circumstances from exercising his authority. The Senior Warden summons the Lodge, but the business of the Lodge, while it is open, is conducted by the Past Master identified in accordance with the Rule, subject to the power of the latter to delegate the duty to another Installed Master who is a member of the Lodge.

Master continuing in office for a second year

From time to time it happens that a Brother continues as Master for a second year, either by the operation of one of the Rules referred to earlier in this chapter or because the Brethren have re-elected him. Brethren are often at a loss as to the procedure to be followed on such an occasion, and indeed there is no one correct

---

3   The word is used of a Lodge in this same sense in Rule 141.

way of dealing with the situation. What follows is an abbreviated version of what I wrote in my earlier book, *Emulation Working Today*,[4] which is in turn based on a note available from the Grand Secretary's Office, headed "NOT OFFICIAL", giving a suggested procedure to meet the situation (but there are other ways of proceeding).

It is quite wrong for an incumbent Master to be reinstalled, as he has not left the Chair, and at his own installation he was obligated and later proclaimed as Master "until the next regular period of election within the Lodge and until a successor shall have been duly elected and installed in his stead".

If the Master has been elected to continue for a second year, the summons will normally include an item such as "To proclaim the Worshipful Master" or "To proclaim W Bro. .... as Master", but merely "To invest the Officers" would not be wrong. If, however, the outgoing Master is continuing because of the provisions of Rules 107 or 108, then the summons, having been issued before the event occurred, will show simply "To install the Master Elect."

There is no need to place Installed Masters in the Wardens' chairs, since there is no Board of Installed Masters on such an occasion, or to replace the Inner Guard. Some Lodges may, however, prefer to do both, either because it is perceived as giving a greater degree of formality to the proceedings or because of a reluctance to leave a Warden's chair temporarily vacant.

As a bare minimum, it is sufficient, with the Lodge still in the first degree, for the Director of Ceremonies to move straight to a point on the mid-line of the Lodge a few paces from the Master's pedestal and with step and sign ask, "Worshipful Master, you having been re-elected as Master of this Lodge (or Worshipful Master, the Master Elect having been prevented by .... from undertaking the office of Master of this Lodge), whom do you appoint your Senior Warden?" The investiture of the Officers then proceeds as normal. It is clearly unnecessary to deliver the address to the Master, but if either of the Wardens has changed since the previous year the address to the Wardens and the address to the Brethren should be delivered. The latter address is directed to all except the Master and Wardens and so, strictly, need not be delivered if neither Warden has changed, but Lodges may wish to deliver it nevertheless to round off the ceremony.

---

4 Lewis Masonic, 2007.

If the reason for the Master continuing in office for a second year is the death of the Master Elect (particularly as for Rule 107 to apply, the death must have occurred less than seven days before the Installation meeting), a Lodge may feel that anything more elaborate than the minimum is inappropriate to the circumstances. In other cases, however, it may wish to adopt a slightly more elaborate procedure. There is no need for the Lodge to be opened beyond the first degree but, again, a Lodge may wish to go up into the third degree to give greater formality to the occasion. If, however, the Lodge is opened into the third degree, it is effectively committed to adopting in the second and first degree whatever procedure it follows in the third.

As there would otherwise have been no point in opening into the third degree, that procedure will inevitably include the proclamation of the Master, probably, though not necessarily, accompanied by a salute by way of greeting and possibly also preceded by the Master Masons passing round the Lodge and saluting him first. There are, however, various permutations of the procedure.

There is no need for the W.Ts. to be presented, and if they are it is better that they should not be explained in full. It is certainly wrong for the Warrant to be presented again to the Master, as it has never left his keeping, and the same applies to the Book of Constitutions, the by-laws and the Hall Stone Jewel (if any). Finally, the Master must not be presented with a Past Master's jewel, as he is not a Past Master until his successor has been installed; the fact that he served for two consecutive years may, however, be recorded on a bar to the jewel.

Death, resignation or protracted absence of Treasurer

If the Treasurer dies or resigns the vacancy is filled in the normal way, in accordance with Rule 121, by election after notice on the summons. This may be done at an emergency meeting. From time to time, however, the Treasurer is away or ill for a prolonged period and this makes it difficult for the Lodge to function, bearing in mind that all cheques must be signed by the Treasurer (and, unless the Lodge resolves otherwise, by one other member as well). In such a situation, Rule 112(b) allows the Lodge to elect what is in effect a deputy Treasurer (which may be either at a regular or an emergency meeting), provided that a dispensation has been granted by the appropriate Masonic authority and notice has been given on the summons in accordance with Rule 112(c). The Brother so elected ceases to have the authority thereby conferred on him once the regularly elected Treasurer is again able to assume his duties, or the next regular period of election, whichever is sooner.

Loss of Warrant

If the Warrant is lost or withheld, either properly by Masonic authority, or improperly by others, the Lodge *cannot meet* until it has been granted a Warrant of Confirmation or the Warrant has been found or restored to it (Rule 103). This is not quite as disastrous as it sounds. Since the period of the Second World War, if not earlier, it has been customary in the case of a lost Warrant, or of one withheld unlawfully, for the Grand Secretary to issue a temporary Warrant of Confirmation, in the form of a letter of authority, bearing the seal of the Grand Lodge, enabling the Lodge to meet. As a matter of practice, it is usual to allow a Lodge to meet under a letter of authority for six months in case the Warrant comes to light within that period, since the cost of a Warrant of Confirmation is considerable (though a prudent Lodge will have its Warrant insured). If the Warrant is subsequently recovered, the Warrant of Confirmation must be returned to the Grand Master.

Premature Passing or Raising

Rule 172 prescribes an interval between degrees of four weeks, and a ceremony carried out in contravention of the Rule is void. It can be validated after the event by a dispensation *nunc pro tunc* (which is charged at double the normal rate for a dispensation). It cannot be authorised in advance, and, as a matter of practice, a validating dispensation is issued only after a full explanation has been given of how the breach came about and the Lodge has shown due contrition for its error. If a dispensation is not granted, the ceremony must be carried out again.

The most common reasons for a breach of the Rule are the incidence of a public holiday and the "farming out" of a ceremony to another Lodge. If the regular date of a meeting falls in the particular year on a prohibited day (Christmas Day, Good Friday or a Sunday) the meeting must be moved to another day.[5] Provided it is not moved by more than seven days either way no dispensation is required, but if the meeting is to be moved by more than seven days (but not more than twenty-eight) a dispensation is necessary. If the meeting falls on a *public holiday* which is not a prohibited day, the seven-day rule also applies (though the Lodge may choose to meet on the day named in the by-laws). Unfortunately, when the seven-day rule is used, the Secretary of a Lodge that meets monthly can be apt to forget that the interval between meetings may be less than twenty-eight

---

5 Rule 139.

days, so that if there is a dearth of candidates the Rule may be breached. When a Lodge farms out work, the Secretary may also fail to count the interval carefully enough, with a similar result.

There is no real excuse in either case, and generally a Secretary who has fallen into the trap is utterly mortified that he has done so. Usually the breach only comes to light when the Secretary applies for a Grand Lodge Certificate, so that if the ceremony carried out in contravention of the Rule was a Passing the dispensation has also to validate the subsequent ceremony of Raising.

By contrast, in a Lodge abroad a dispensation may be granted in advance to authorise an interval of not less than one week.

Master of more than one Lodge

Rule 115 provides that a Brother may not be Master of more than one Lodge at a time without a dispensation, which must be granted by the Grand Master, except that if the Lodges are in the same District, the District Grand Master is permitted to grant it.[6] The dispensation is required to authorise the Installation, not the election (unlike a dispensation under Rule 109), and cannot be granted until the Brother concerned has been both installed in the Chair of one Lodge and elected to the Chair of the other. As a matter of practice, a dispensation is hardly ever refused for a second Chair and virtually never granted for a third. The dispensation has to be obtained (and paid for) by the second Lodge and the need for it can occasionally cause considerable annoyance in a Lodge, which may not be pleased to find that the Master Elect has not told the Secretary or anyone else that he is already in, or elected to, the Chair of another Lodge. The Rule, however, can be quite arbitrary in the way that the expense falls, because it can easily happen that because of the pattern of meetings in the respective Lodges, in between his election and his Installation in one Lodge a Brother may be both elected and installed in the Chair of another Lodge.

Prevention of a meeting

The quorum – the minimum number – required for a meeting of a Lodge to be held is five, apart from the Tyler and the candidate, of whom two must be members of the Lodge and one an Installed Master (see *Information for the*

---

6   This is a hangover from an earlier age when communication was much slower. In these days of rapid communication the exception is outmoded, but continues to exist for the time being.

Guidance of Members of the Craft). The Installed Master does not have to be a member of the Lodge, but if he is not, and neither of the Wardens is present, then it is suggested that the effect of Rule 119 is to require one of the members of the Lodge to act as Senior Warden for the occasion and to conduct the business of the Lodge. It should also be noted that if, but only if, there is no Installed Master under the English Constitution present, an Installed Master under the Irish or Scottish Constitution may be requested by the Officer in charge of the Lodge to perform any ceremony which the Warden is not competent to perform. If only five Brethren are present, then the administrative business of the Lodge can be transacted, but neither a Passing nor a Raising may take place (since the candidate will be one of the five), though an initiation may (since the candidate, not being a Mason, will have been disregarded for the purpose of counting the quorum), and so may the Installation, provided that there are three Installed Masters present (apart from the Master Elect and the Tyler). If only three Installed Masters are present, including the Tyler, he may legitimately[7] be one of the Board of Installed Masters, while one of the Master Masons acts as Tyler.

If the required quorum is not present, the Lodge may not be opened and the meeting must be abandoned. A statement must be entered in the Minute Book recording the fact. The formula suggested is: "The meeting of the Lodge on Monday 2nd February, 2009 was duly called in accordance with the attached summons. Owing to adverse weather conditions[8] the required number of Brethren to open the Lodge could not be assembled and the meeting was abandoned." It should be particularly noted that a meeting *may not be cancelled* in advance of the day or time of the meeting; it may only be abandoned in the light of circumstances prevailing at the time for which it has been summoned.

The members of a Lodge should not be concerned, if a meeting is abandoned, that it will affect the Lodge's continuity of working when it comes to establishing its entitlement to a Centenary or Bi-Centenary Warrant (see Chapter 11). It is only if a Lodge fails to meet for a whole year (and thereby renders itself liable to be erased – Rule 189) that continuity is regarded as having been broken.[9] Though only minor inconvenience is likely to flow in most cases from the abandonment

---

7 Except, perhaps, if he is an unattached Mason.
8 Or, for example, "a rail strike" or "terrorist action" (or as the case may be).
9 In any event, the Grand Master has the discretion to disregard a break in working if it is the result of *force majeure*. A classic instance is of Lodges in the Province of Jersey which were prevented from meeting from January 1941 until August 1945.

of a single meeting, it is more disruptive if the lost meeting is the one named in the Lodge's by-laws for the election or the Installation of the Master. In the latter case the position is governed by Rule 108, and it is merely necessary to install the Master within five weeks. In the former, the case should be treated as falling within Rule 106, as though the Master Elect had died or become disqualified. An amendment to the Rule that will place the matter beyond doubt is currently (April 2009) before the Grand Lodge, and may be expected to be in force by the time this book is published.

Bad behaviour

Even Freemasons misbehave from time to time. At one level they fail to pay their subscriptions or make themselves so unpopular with their Brethren that the latter want no more to do with them. Rule 181 enables a Lodge to exclude Brethren permanently for "sufficient cause". The process of exclusion has already been dealt with in Chapter 3, and I would only reiterate the point that it requires a majority of two-thirds of the members *present*.

On a different level altogether are Brethren who fall foul of the criminal law. Any Brother who breaks the law is technically guilty of a Masonic offence: "As a citizen every Freemason has a duty not to engage in conduct which is contrary to the law of the land. As a Freemason he also has a duty not to engage in activity which may bring Freemasonry into disrepute." – Rule 179. A Freemason convicted of an offence for which he is sentenced to a term of imprisonment (including a suspended sentence), or in respect of whom a Community Order is made by a Court in the United Kingdom, or who is placed on a sex offenders' register in accordance with certain Acts of Parliament, or who is convicted of an offence involving dishonesty or violence, is obliged by Rule 179A to report the conviction to the Master of his Lodge within twenty-eight days (or, if he is unattached, to the Grand Secretary). The Master must then within a further twenty-eight days report it in turn to the Metropolitan, Provincial or District Grand Secretary (or otherwise to the Grand Secretary). The Master has a further duty to report similarly any other case that is likely to bring Freemasonry into disrepute. The Metropolitan, Provincial or District Grand Secretary must transmit it promptly to the Grand Secretary, and report to him any other conduct by a Brother that in the opinion of the Metropolitan, Provincial or District Grand Master is likely to bring Freemasonry into disrepute. Meanwhile the Brother who has been convicted, *whether or not he has complied with his duty to report it*, is precluded from attending any Lodge or Chapter without the written permission of the Masonic authority under whom the

Lodge or Chapter falls until his case has been determined by Masonic authority.

It will thus be seen that a Brother suffering a conviction falling within the Rule is all but suspended until his case has been resolved in Masonic disciplinary proceedings. On the other hand, a Brother convicted of an offence not within the Rule, or who is, for example, struck off by his professional body, or who has committed a purely Masonic offence, does not have to report the matter or to abstain from Masonic activity. He may, however, find himself on the receiving end of an invitation from his Metropolitan, Provincial or District Grand Master not to attend Lodges or Chapters. He is not obliged to comply with the invitation, but if he fails to do so and misconduct is subsequently established, the failure is likely to be taken into account in arriving at the Masonic penalty to be imposed.

10

MISCELLANEOUS

1. The … headings are for convenience of reference only, and are not to affect the construction of these Laws and Regulations nor to form any part thereof.

Rule 1, Book of Constitutions

This is a chapter intended to draw together a number of disparate threads which do not necessarily (or at all) have any particular connection with each other, but each of which is deserving of a mention in its own right.

Over the years Freemasonry has accumulated a good number of strange little quirks and customs – and which is a quirk and which is a custom may be for the individual reader to judge.

The Volume of the Sacred Law

Some workings prescribe a particular point at which the Bible is to be opened according to the particular degree in which the Lodge is working, and some Lodges have bookmarks of varying degrees of complexity to mark the passages concerned. It goes without saying that a Brother whose Lodge's working prescribes such particular passages should adhere scrupulously to the custom of the Lodge. It should, however, be noted that neither in the Grand Lodge nor in Emulation Working are any such passages prescribed, and that in both the primary consideration is to ensure that the Bible is opened as near as may be to the middle, to ensure that there is an equal number of pages on each side so that the square and compasses do not slide about on the Book.

"Reigning Masters"

A particular *bête noire* of many Brethren – I am one of them – is the description of those who are currently the Worshipful Masters of their Lodge as "reigning

Masters".[1] They are simply "Masters" or "Worshipful Masters"; if they are not current Masters, they are Past Masters, so that the word "reigning" is redundant. This is probably a good example of the tendency, noted earlier, to regard a formula or procedure that is more elaborate and pompous as inherently better. The Master of a Lodge is not the Monarch; he does not reign over his Lodge, even though he rules and directs it.

Amalgamations

There is a long history in the Craft of two Lodges amalgamating into a single one and, generally, working thereafter under the Warrant of the older Lodge – or at any rate the Lodge with the lower number. Such "informal" amalgamations have been treated as genuine unions or mergers and the Lodges have been accepted as having continuity of working (if they do have continuity – or uninterrupted working) from the date of Consecration of the older Lodge, even if a Lodge now works under the Warrant of the newer Lodge. Since 2000, however, the practice has been formalised by the grant of a Certificate of Amalgamation, reciting the origins of the participating Lodges and recording their union. Another new feature introduced at the same time was the return to the continuing Lodge of the cancelled Warrant of an Amalgamating Lodge, to be held with and exhibited at the same times as the Warrant of the continuing Lodge. A Centenary or Bi-Centenary Warrant held by the Amalgamating Lodge also continues in existence for the benefit of all the members of the continuing Lodge. Similarly if the Amalgamating Lodge has a Hall Stone Jewel, but the continuing Lodge does not, that too is transferred to the latter; if, however, both are Hall Stone Lodges, only one jewel will be needed, and that of the Amalgamating Lodge must be returned to the Grand Master (as is the case when a Lodge is erased in the normal way).

The Initiate

An initiate has always been regarded as someone special, and at dinner is seated on the immediate right of the Master, taking precedence even of the Grand Master should he be present. In the Lodge, at the end of the ceremony he is to be seated in the north-east, on the immediate right of the Senior Deacon, and not, as used to be the custom in some old Lodges, on the immediate right of the Master. Similarly, he is not entitled to any precedence in an outgoing procession. (See *Information for the Guidance of Members of the Craft*.)

---

1 This has occasionally led some wag to suggest that the collective noun for them is a "shower".

Grand Lodge Certificates

Originally the Grand Lodge Certificate was devised to prevent spurious Masons imposing on the charity of Lodges and their members. Many different designs were used during the eighteenth and early nineteenth centuries, but the current design has been in use, essentially unchanged, since 1819. A Brother is entitled to a Grand Lodge Certificate on being registered as having been raised to the third degree, provided he is in good standing (Rule 174). In special circumstances, a first or second degree certificate (which is in reality a letter signed by the Grand Secretary, or the Assistant Grand Secretary on his behalf) may be issued to a Brother, which he may exchange for a normal Grand Lodge Certificate in due course. As a matter of practice, an interim certificate is normally only issued to enable a Brother to join another Lodge when he has ceased to belong to his mother Lodge.[2]

A Grand Lodge Certificate should be presented in open Lodge (and the fact recorded in the minutes); if that is not practicable it must be sent to the Brother by registered post[3] and the fact reported to the Lodge at the next meeting by the Secretary (and recorded in the minutes). In either case the Brother must sign the certificate in the margin immediately on receiving it. A Brother visiting a Lodge where he is not known should carry his Certificate with him and, conversely, a Lodge should not admit as a visitor an unknown Brother without seeing his Certificate. A Brother is required to produce his Certificate on joining another Lodge, or in order to become a member of the Royal Arch (or of other Masonic Orders). If a Grand Lodge Certificate is lost, a replacement can be obtained on payment of the prescribed fee.

Music

Music can greatly enhance any Masonic ceremony. Unfortunately, if used insensitively it can detract from it just as much. Music is supposed to be one of the seven liberal –

---

2 In those circumstances, because of the operation of Rule 127, he almost invariably cannot be Passed and Raised by request (under Rule 173) in the Lodge he wishes to join.

3 "Rules 174, 175, 181, and 185, Book of Constitutions, require documents to be sent by Registered Post which is expensive. The rules aim to ensure that documents have been delivered at an address rather than to ensure their safety in transit, and in March 1963 Grand Lodge agreed that the words 'registered post' in the Rules quoted above and related rules should be deemed to include recorded delivery. The Board believes it timely to draw attention to this ruling, with the modification that delivery is only certain under the Recorded Delivery system if the additional 'Advice of Delivery' service is used, and steps taken to ensure that the advice of delivery is rendered." (Extract from Report of Board of General Purposes, adopted 10 March 1982.)

not deadly – arts and sciences. Nowadays far fewer Brethren have skills on the piano, let alone the organ, than used to be the case, and though the level of actual competence required in a Lodge Organist is relatively modest and undemanding, it is not always to be found amongst a Lodge's members. In my earlier book[4] I wrote:

"In these days when Brethren capable of playing a keyboard instrument are increasingly hard to find, many Lodges rely on the services of a visitor who, either for love or for a fee, is willing to discharge the Organist's duties. It is perfectly proper for such a Brother to wear the Organist's collar while acting in the office. If he regularly acts as such, and the Lodge wishes to acknowledge his contribution by listing him on the summons, he must not, however, appear in the normal place in the list of Officers (Rule 104 of the Book of Constitutions precludes a Brother who is not a subscribing member from holding any office in the Lodge except that of Tyler), but should be placed below the Tyler and be described as "Acting Organist" or "Visiting Organist". Similarly he may not be invested in the office during the ceremony of Installation, though there can be no objection to the Master asking the Director of Ceremonies to conduct him to him at the end of the Installation and entrusting (but not investing) him with the collar with a few appropriate words."

It should go without saying that a visiting Organist, particularly if he is being paid a fee for his services, should be at pains to ensure that whatever he plays will fit in with the Lodge's established practice, and should ensure that he takes advice in advance from the Master, Director of Ceremonies or Secretary.

There is more to the art of being a good Organist than might appear. A Brother does not need to be a Fellow of the Royal College of Organists to qualify; what is most important is the ability to shape discreet background music to the requirements of the ceremonies and other parts of the Lodge's meetings. If, however, a Lodge does not have a Brother who meets that level of skill, and does not wish to secure the services of a guest Organist, it is better to dispense with music altogether.

Vocal music during the ceremonies is found much less frequently now than was once the case. This may be partly the result of a change in fashion, for the opening and closing hymns still seem to be sung with gusto, but it is also partly the result of the edict of the Grand Lodge that "care must be taken that vocal music is such that

---

4 *Emulation Working Today* – Lewis Masonic, 2007.

it is not identified exclusively with a particular form of divine worship and that it does not offend the susceptibilities of a particular creed since Masonry is open to the adherents of every faith which requires a belief in a Supreme Being, and that all other items should be scrutinized with the same care as any spoken additions, thus preventing innovations in the body of Masonry and bringing to an end any that may have developed."[5] Vocal music must therefore be used in Masonic ceremonies only with the sanction of the Metropolitan, Provincial or District Grand Master (or the Grand Master in the case of unattached Lodges).

Lodge emblems, logos, banners and badges

Most Lodges have adopted distinctive badges or designs which are used, for example, on the Lodge's headed paper, Past Master's jewel, and banner. In the case of jewels, Rule 241 governs the situation (see Chapter 2). In relation to designs generally, the Board of General Purposes reported in March 1996:

'The Board wishes to remind Brethren of the requirement in Rule 241, Book of Constitutions, that the designs of jewels must have been approved or allowed by the MW The Grand Master. By long-standing custom, and for similar reasons approval is also required for any design used as the emblem of a Lodge, whether on summonses, Lodge stationery, or as a Lodge banner. Notes for guidance on designs are available from the Grand Secretary's office.'

The notes referred to (which should be obtained via the relevant Metropolitan, Provincial or District Grand Secretary) are not exhaustive. In summary, they restrict the use of heraldic devices (and in particular the Royal Arms and those of the United Grand Lodge of England), and prohibit the use of religious symbols, the Imperial Crown or a wreath of corn and acacia (the last being the emblem of Grand Rank).

The Board of Installed Masters

As seen in the previous chapter, three Installed Masters are required in order to form a Board of Installed Masters and carry out the Inner Working of the Ceremony of Installation. This is an appropriate point at which to dispel a couple of possible misconceptions.

---

5 See *Information for the Guidance of Members of the Craft* – "Vocal Music in Degree Ceremonies".

First, as to the word "Board": the use of this is strictly limited, being permissible only for the Board of Installed Masters, the Board of Grand Stewards of Grand Lodge, the Board of General Purposes of Grand Lodge, and District Boards of General Purposes or of Benevolence. Any other use of the word (usually as a substitute for "Committee") is strictly prohibited. So, for example, it is wrong to refer to a Provincial Board of Grand Stewards (quite apart from the fact that the duties of Provincial and District Grand Stewards are essentially different from those of the Grand Stewards) or to a Board of Inquiry (for a disciplinary committee).

Secondly, the words near the beginning of the Installation ceremony "He must have been regularly elected ... and presented to a Board of Installed Masters that he may receive... Bro. ...., you having been so elected and presented..." have over the years given rise to more misunderstanding than most in the ritual. In order to comply with what they took to be an injunction in the ritual, some Lodges took to holding a separate meeting of the Master and Past Masters, at which the Master Elect could be "presented" (or introduced) to those there assembled, either prior to, or earlier on, the day of the Installation. Alternatively, Brethren, recognising that such a prior meeting is inappropriate, have suggested that the words in the ritual are wrong and should be changed. In fact, the Board of Installed Masters is formed at the moment when Installed Masters are placed in the Wardens' Chairs before the Lodge is opened, or resumed, in the second degree. The Board, thus formed, is later formally constituted, after the Master Masons have retired, at the beginning of the Inner Working. The former practice was unequivocally disapproved of by the Grand Lodge in 1973:

"The Board of Installed Masters has no other function [than that of installing the Master] and cannot by any pretext be opened at any other time or occasion. ... Any idea that a Board of Installed Masters should or may be held prior to the day of installation or as part of any earlier ceremony on that day is quite erroneous, and where such practice exists it should cease."

Thirdly, the Immediate Past Master is invested as part of the Inner Working of the Board of Installed Masters, and if absent from the Installation meeting cannot be invested on a later occasion. He is, of course, Immediate Past Master by virtue of having served as the previous Master, and needs no formal investiture to confirm him in that position (and, under Rule 104(e), reoccupies it if his successor dies or ceases in some other way to be a member of the Lodge while holding the position of Immediate Past Master).

In 1966 the Board of General Purposes gave guidance on the eligibility of Brethren of other Constitutions to attend the Inner Working of the Board of Installed Masters:

"The Board feels that the fact of being installed as Master of a regular Lodge should be the paramount consideration and should outweigh variations of method of installation, being encouraged in this belief by the recollection that the obligation of secrecy taken in the first degree covers equally all secrets subsequently communicated.

"It therefore suggests to the Grand Lodge that any member in good standing of a recognised Constitution (a full list of all such bodies being given in the current Masonic Year Book) who can satisfactorily prove that he is or has been Master of a Lodge should be permitted to attend the Inner Working of the Installation Ceremony.[6] Where such proof is solely documentary it must include convincing evidence of identity, but lack of knowledge of such signs, tokens, and words as are communicated in Boards of Installed Masters of English Lodges should not debar an Installed Master from remaining present at a Board of Installed Masters."

Whilst any Installed Master from a recognised Constitution is thus entitled to attend the Inner Working of the Board of Installed Masters, it is less clear that all are to be counted towards the quorum if the attendance is sparse. The concordat with the Grand Lodges of Ireland and Scotland expressly provides that:

"In each of the three jurisdictions, a duly installed Master under either of the other Constitutions shall, if not otherwise disqualified, be entitled to be present at a Board of Installed Masters, and to form one of the quorum; but not to preside therein or to instal a Master, unless requested to do so by the Board. Nor can a Visiting Master or Past Master of another Constitution preside in the Lodge he is visiting. In case there is not present a Master or a Past Master duly qualified under the home jurisdiction, then and then only the Officer in charge of the Lodge may request a Master or Past Master under one of the other two Constitutions to perform any ceremony which the Warden is not competent to perform. This agreement is not to interfere with the right of the Worshipful

---

6 To these must be added "certain Brethren who hold high rank in the Scandinavian system ... about whose eligibility to attend any question should be addressed to the Grand Secretary". (Extract from Report of Board of General Purposes, adopted 9 March 1966.)

Master of a Lodge to invite a Member of the Lodge or a visiting Master or Past Master of any of the three Constitutions to perform any ceremony without assuming the Chair."

This strongly suggests that despite the inclusiveness of the wording quoted above, not every Installed Master entitled to remain present should be included in the quorum. In practice the situation is most unlikely ever to arise, but there is a theoretical possibility that on the day of Installation there might be present only a single Irish or Scottish Installed Master and two Installed Masters from Constitutions which have no esoteric Inner Working. In such a case, it is suggested that the Installation would have to be abandoned for want of a proper quorum.

Lodges of Instruction

Far fewer Lodges these days have a duly sanctioned Lodge of Instruction, and far fewer Brethren attend such Lodges of Instruction as do exist, whether that of their own Lodge or that of another Lodge which is willing to take (as many do) members of other Lodges. This is a great pity. Not only do Lodges of Instruction have a thoroughly beneficial effect on the standard of a Lodge's working, but, as many Brethren will testify, it is often in the Lodge of Instruction that the strongest and most enduring Masonic friendships are made.

Lodges of Instruction are regulated by Rules 132 to 135 of the Book of Constitutions. Those Rules are both clear and succinct. There are, however, a few points worth noting. First, that the sanction for a Lodge of Instruction, once given under Rule 132 continues in force until it is withdrawn in accordance with Rule 135; the item sometimes seen on a Lodge summons, that the Lodge continue to sanction a Lodge of Instruction for the ensuing year, is therefore misconceived. Secondly, that although the Grand Master has power to grant a licence to a Lodge of Instruction himself, he has never yet exercised that power.[7] Finally, that although the Books and papers of a Lodge of Instruction become, on its dissolution, the property of the sanctioning Lodge, its other property does not; correspondingly, the sanctioning Lodge has no formal responsibility for the debts or other liabilities of the Lodge of Instruction, either during its lifetime or after it has ceased to exist (though the existence of undischarged debts during its lifetime would undoubtedly afford grounds for withdrawing the sanction).

---

7   To the best of my knowledge, the only occasion on which such a licence has been sought was in March 1830, by Emulation Lodge of Improvement, when the request was declined.

11

ADMINISTRATIVE MATTERS

Ashes to ashes and dust to dust;
If no one else does it the Secretary must.

Colin Dyer – *One Hundred Years of Quatuor Coronati Lodge*

This chapter, like the last, deals with miscellaneous matters, but in this case the matters are of a specifically administrative rather than a general nature. It therefore deals with words rather than with actions and things, and with the written word rather than the spoken.

Masonic styles, titles, offices and ranks

First, a quick guide to the nomenclature, something which many get wrong.

The correct prefixes are set out in Rule 6. These go with the *rank* held by a Brother, though "Very Worshipful" and above *can* be applied to the office held. The latter usage, except in the case of the Rulers of the Craft, is rarely met with today, so that, for example, the form "The Very Worshipful Grand Secretary, Right Worshipful Brother Sir James Stubbs" is all but extinct. It has always been wrong to refer to me as "The Very Worshipful Assistant Grand Secretary"; I am either "The Assistant Grand Secretary, Very Worshipful Brother Graham Redman" or "Very Worshipful Brother Graham Redman, Assistant Grand Secretary".

For the Rulers of the Craft, the correct styles are as in the toast list set out in Chapter 13:

The Most Worshipful The Grand Master, His Royal Highness The Duke
of Kent, *KG, GCMG, GCVO, ADC*
The Most Worshipful Pro Grand Master, Peter Geoffrey Lowndes

The Right Worshipful Deputy Grand Master, Jonathan Spence
The Right Worshipful Assistant Grand Master, David Kenneth Williamson

with the alternatives:

MW Bro. His Royal Highness The Duke of Kent, *KG, GCMG, GCVO, ADC,* Grand Master

and so on.

The order in which the Grand Officers and other members of the Grand Lodge rank among themselves is set out at length in Rule 5. It should be noted that in the case of any Grand Office or rank which is qualified by "Deputy", "Assistant", "Senior" or "Junior", the adjective always *precedes* the word "Grand", *e.g.* "Senior Grand Deacon", and in the case of a past rank, the word "Past" of course precedes all others.[1]

This is mirrored at Metropolitan, Provincial and District level, with "Metropolitan", "Provincial" or "District" preceding what would be the style of the office in the Grand Lodge; so it is "Provincial Senior Grand Warden", not "Senior Provincial Grand Warden" and "Provincial Deputy Grand Secretary", not "Deputy Provincial Grand Secretary". By way of exception, at almost the highest level "Deputy Provincial Grand Master" and "Assistant Metropolitan Grand Master" are the correct styles, but these are perhaps best looked at on the basis that the title "Provincial Grand Master" (which is an office in Grand Lodge) is a single, indivisible string of words so that "Deputy" or "Assistant" can only properly precede the entire string. There is another small quirk at Metropolitan, Provincial and District level, in that a Metropolitan, Provincial or District Master is described as "for", but *any other* Metropolitan, Provincial or District Grand Officer is described as "of", the Metropolitan Area, Province or District: thus it is "the Provincial Grand Master *for* Bedfordshire", but "the Deputy Provincial Grand Master *of* Bedfordshire".

Abbreviations

Abbreviation is to some extent a matter of personal taste, and over the years,

---

1 This is in contrast to the Mark degree, where "Senior" and "Junior" follow "Grand", e.g. "Grand Senior Deacon".

fashions have changed. Thus fifty years ago the accepted abbreviation for Grand Standard Bearer was G.St.B. It is now GStB. I must confess to an old-fashioned preference for the use of the full stop to indicate an abbreviation, but I no longer feel able to indulge that preference in my working life. Far more regrettable, however, is the growing trend away from separating abbreviations with a comma, sometimes substituting a full stop, sometimes merely leaving a space, and sometimes mixing commas, full stops and spaces, apparently indiscriminately. There is a useful note at the end of the alphabetical list of Grand Officers published annually in the *Masonic Year Book*:

"The method of abbreviation of Grand and Past Grand Rank used in the Masonic Year Book should be followed whenever it is necessary to abbreviate a Masonic Rank.

"In Provincial or District Grand Ranks, 'Provincial' or 'District' should be abbreviated to 'Prov' or 'Dist' except that where space is short 'Pr' is acceptable for 'Provincial'."

Nonetheless, there is scope for variation. What there must not be is ambiguity, and what there ought not to be is inconsistency. Thus, it is suggested, the abbreviation of Provincial to P (rather than Prov – or at least Pr)[2] is wrong because of ambiguity, just as is the abbreviation of District to D (rather than Dist). Bad habits, however, become ingrained, and it is probably now impossible to eradicate the misuse of PGM, which is properly the abbreviation for Past Grand Master, to refer (particularly in speech, but increasingly in writing) to a Provincial Grand Master. At the present time, because there are currently no Past Grand Masters, it satisfies the ambiguity test, though not the consistency test.

Honours, qualifications and ranks in summonses, etc

The subject of abbreviations leads naturally on to that of showing various designations in summonses, lists of members, and Year Books. In the case of the first two this is very much a matter of a Lodge's custom. Whilst there might be

---

2 In some Provinces "Prov" is used to indicate the fact that the individual has held the active office, and the shorter "Pr" to show that he received the past rank.

no compelling reason to show more than Masonic designations, it is proper to include honours and decorations as well, and it is certainly wrong not to show titles. The order in which items should be shown after the Masonic prefix (*e.g.* "W Bro.") is:

1. Titles and prefixes
2. Name
3. Orders (or Honours)
4. Decorations (except for *VC* and *GC*, which precede all Honours etc, other than the designation *Bt* – or, less commonly nowadays, *Bart* – for a baronet)
5. Appointments, such as *QHP, QC* and *DL*
6. Degrees
7. Professional qualifications
8. Letters denoting membership of one of the Services (*RN, RNR, RM, RAF*)
9. Masonic offices and ranks (in descending order – see below).

Notes:

1. Peerages and knighthoods should always be included, the former with the appropriate prefix,[3] as must courtesy titles and courtesy styles denoting the son of a peer. A Privy Councillor should always be accorded his prefix "The Rt. Hon.". (See 5 below for peers who are also Privy Councillors.) Clergymen should, if they wish (some non-stipendiary clergy do not), be designated by "The Rev.", and the higher clergy – or at least those of the Established Church – by the appropriate variation thereon. The prefix "Dr." gives rise to rather more difficulty: strictly it should only be used by those who hold a doctorate from a university, but it is also widely used to denote a physician, who may indeed hold a doctorate, but is more likely to be a Bachelor of Medicine and Bachelor of Surgery; in the latter case it is better not used if the custom of the Lodge is to show degrees as well as honours and decorations. By contrast, in some universities a Doctor of Philosophy may choose not to use the prefix "Dr.", which is reserved by purists for those who have received one of the

---

3 His Grace the Duke of Devonshire (the fuller form "The Most Noble the Duke of Devonshire" is almost, but not quite, obsolete); The Most Hon. the Marquess of Northampton; The Rt. Hon. the Earl of Eglinton and Winton (but N.B.: The Rt. Hon. the Earl Cadogan); The Rt. Hon. the Viscount Gough; The Rt. Hon. Lord Lane of Horsell.

higher doctorates. Naval, Military and Air Force ranks are generally a matter for the individual. Except in a Service Lodge, a rank below Major or its equivalent would not normally be used by a retired Officer, and it is generally considered "poor form" for even that or a higher rank to be used by a member of one of the reserve forces.

2. Whatever the complexities of prefixes, titles, orders and decorations, it might be thought that at least the name of a Brother would be straightforwardness itself. Even this simple element, however, may require care in the handling. If a decision has been made to limit each entry to initials and surname, to conform to current usage a knight or baronet should still be distinguished by his preferred forename, as *must* the younger son of a Duke or Marquess; a peer should have no initials, but may need a territorial designation to distinguish him from another peer of the same grade with the same name (*e.g.* the late Lord Lane of Horsell). If forenames are printed in full, some means might be used to indicate the Brother's preferred forename if it is not his first – perhaps by underlining it or placing the other forename(s) within brackets.

3. and 4. There is a strict order in which letters denoting honours and decorations must be shown.[4]

5. There is also a strict order for Appointments,[5] but while it must be strictly adhered to if these are included, it is not necessary that any or all of them should be shown, except for *PC*, which should always be used in the case of a peer, if applicable, as it is the means of distinguishing a peer who is a Privy Councillor from one who is not (the prefix Rt. Hon., which is the normal way of showing membership of the Privy Council, being ambiguous in the

---

4   The following list covers most, but recourse should be had, if necessary, to a work such as *Debrett's Correct Form*, as it is not possible in part of a single short chapter to cover every option:
    Bt; VC, GC; KG, KT, GCB, OM, GCSI, GCMG, GCIE, GCVO, GBE, CH, KCB, KCSI, KCMG, KCIE, KCVO, KBE, CB, CSI, CMG, CIE, CVO, CBE, DSO, LVO, OBE, ISO, MVO, MBE; IOM (Mil), RRC, DSC, MC, DFC, AFC, ARRC, OBI, DCM, CGM, GM, DCM, IDSM, DSM, MM, DFM, AFM, SGM, IOM, CPM, QGM, BEM, KPM, KPFSM, QPM, QFSM, CPM, MSM, ERD, VD, TD, ED, RD, VRD, AE, CD.
5   *PC, ADC, QHP, QHS, QHDS, QHC; QC, JP, DL; MP.*

case of a peer). Although *JP* appears in the footnote, it is not the current practice of the Grand Lodge to show the abbreviation in the *Masonic Year Book* or other documents, to the periodic annoyance of some Brethren so entitled. This is, however, a matter of practice in the Grand Secretary's Office, and Metropolitan Areas, Provinces, Districts and Private Lodges are free to adopt their own policy.

6. Degrees are not currently included in entries in the *Masonic Year Book* etc, but the same observation applies as in the case of *JP*. They, like Orders and Decorations, are subject to a strict order, which varies according to the particular university (*e.g.* Oxford shows them in ascending order, Cambridge in descending).

7. Professional qualifications are not currently included in entries in the *Masonic Year Book* etc, and may be unlikely to be included elsewhere, except in the case of the better known, such as *FRCS*, *FCA* or *FRICS*.

8. Service designations are important in the case of certain ranks, the most notable being Captain, which is a far more senior rank in the Royal Navy than in the Royal Marines or the Army.

9. Abbreviations of Masonic ranks etc should be shown in the following order:

(a)   OSM, where applicable;

(b)   the Grand Office or Rank, if any, which establishes the Brother's position in the table in Rule 5 of the Book of Constitutions and therefore his prefix under Rule 6;

(c)   any lower ranking Grand Office;[6]

---

6   Although Rule 25 prohibits the holding of more than one office in Grand Lodge at one and the same time, the same rule allows a Metropolitan, Provincial or District Grand Master or a Grand Steward to hold one other office in addition thereto. In the event, therefore, that I were permitted while still in the employment of the Grand Lodge to serve a second term as a Grand Steward, my designation would be "PGSwdB, AGSec, GStwd".

(d)   the Metropolitan, Provincial, District or Overseas equivalents to (b) and (c) relevant to the particular summons, List of Members, or Year Book;

(e)   if desired, and if it is the custom of the Lodge, the Metropolitan, Provincial, District or Overseas equivalents to (b) and (c) in other Metropolitan Areas, Provinces, Districts or Lodges abroad not under Districts, but clearly distinguished as such (*e.g.* "PProvSGD, Essex", alternatively "PProvSGD (Essex)") except in the case of Metropolitan and Overseas Ranks, where there is no scope for ambiguity. There is no overriding protocol as to the order in which these should be shown if a Brother has such a rank in more than one area, as none confers any precedence outside the relevant area, though some would hold that Overseas Ranks should appear first as they are conferred directly by the Grand Master, followed by Metropolitan Ranks, since a Metropolitan Grand Master ranks above Provincial and District Grand Masters (and a Metropolitan Rank might, in any case, have been conferred by the Grand Master before October 2003). In practice, it is probably best to show them in descending order of seniority;

(f)   if desired, and if it is the custom of the Lodge, any rank under another recognised Grand Lodge, again clearly distinguished as such, preferably by showing it in brackets, *e.g.* "(PJGW, Grande Loge Nationale Française)".

It should not be lost sight of that the above list sets out the *order* in which non-Masonic and Masonic designations should be shown; it is not intended to lay down any rule as to what *should* be shown in any particular situation. Items 1 to 4 in the list will almost invariably be included – but not necessarily every particular item within them. Item 5 will generally be included, but items 6 and 7 rarely. Which of the Masonic designations at item 9 are shown is generally a matter of the custom of the Lodge concerned, particularly those relating to other Provinces or Constitutions. As a matter of etiquette it would be wrong for a Brother entitled to one of those designations to make a fuss if the custom of his Lodge was against showing it.

The word "designate"

This should be used very sparingly. The very fact that it is used indicates clearly that the individual is not yet entitled to the title that precedes it. Properly, it is used in the Craft only to indicate an appointment made by the Grand Master which has not yet become effective, *i.e.* Metropolitan, Provincial or District Grand Master, Grand Inspector[7] or the first Master and Wardens of a new Lodge; and its *formal* use is restricted to the printed Order of Procedure and other documents issued in connection with the ceremony, and in the ceremony itself, in which the individual concerned will be installed or invested in the new office. There can be no real objection to referring to someone as the Master designate of a new Lodge, even long in advance of the Consecration, but as a matter of etiquette, it is wrong to refer to a Brother as, for example, Provincial Grand Master designate while his predecessor is still in office. Even after the death or retirement of the previous incumbent, if the successor is the Deputy Provincial Grand Master, it is strictly correct to refer to him as the Deputy Provincial Grand Master in Charge, which is not only his official title (see Rule 64, Book of Constitutions) but is the capacity in which he exercises authority during the interregnum (whereas the Brother appointed, if he is not the Deputy, has only one power that he can exercise before he is installed, namely to summon Provincial Grand Lodge for the purposes of his installation).

In this connection, it is certainly wrong to refer to a Brother (as I once heard an Assistant Provincial Grand Master introduced at meeting of a Lodge to which he was paying an official visit) as "Deputy Provincial Grand Master designate".

Name of a Lodge

Rule 98 provides that every Lodge must be distinguished by a name or title, as well as a number, and that no Lodge may make any alteration in its name without the approval of the Grand Master, and, in a Metropolitan Area, Province or District, that of the Metropolitan, Provincial or District Grand Master also.

As a matter of practice, the Grand Master's advisers are unwilling to support a name which is that of a living or deceased Freemason below the rank of a Metropolitan, Provincial or District Grand Master, though they may be willing in a suitable case to support a name which is that of a famous person (not a Freemason – or even necessarily a man) who is dead (a recent example is Sir

---

7 A Grand Inspector is not formally installed, but operates by virtue of his patent of appointment; in strict usage, therefore, the word is inappropriate and its use should be confined to oral shorthand for a successor whose appointment has been announced before the retirement of the present incumbent.

Edward Elgar Lodge, No. 9837). It probably follows from this that a more junior Freemason who had acquired fame for some other reason might, at least after his death, have a Lodge named after him.

A Lodge that seeks to change its name will need to make a good case for the change, giving the reasoning that underlies it, and also to show that the change has the support of the great majority of its members. The most common reason at the present time for a change of name being requested is that two or more Lodges have amalgamated; in such a situation it is often (but by no means invariably) desired to mark the union by adopting a new name which combines, or otherwise reflects, the separate names of the component Lodges. The Grand Master's advisers are generally sympathetic to such requests, but are reluctant to recommend any name that is unduly long (as a rule of thumb, six words should be the absolute maximum) or which combines the separate elements in an inappropriate way.

Name of a Brother

For one reason or another, the name which appears on a Brother's Grand Lodge Certificate sometimes needs to be changed. This may be for various reasons. At one extreme, the Brother may have been incorrectly registered, sometimes (though rarely) as the result of a mistake in the Grand Secretary's Office, but far more often because the Registration Form has been filled in incorrectly by or on behalf of a candidate (commonly with incomplete or abbreviated forenames); at the other extreme are those elevated to the peerage. In between are those who have voluntarily changed their names by deed poll, statutory declaration or other means. The Book of Constitutions provides for the same fee to be levied for amending a Grand Lodge Certificate as for a replacement certificate, but the fee for amendment has customarily been waived for many years. This is not at all logical, since the amount of time in the Grand Secretary's Office spent on an amendment is generally rather greater than that spent on a simple replacement.

Certification on Registration Forms

Every Registration Form requires (apart from the signatures of the candidate, his proposer and his seconder to their respective declarations) the completion and signature of at least two further certificates that it contains.

Before the candidate is proposed in open Lodge, and certainly before the ballot is taken, the certificate of the Master at the foot of the third page should have been signed. It is still all too common for that certificate not to be read out, as required, before the ballot is taken, and even for the Secretary to send the form up to the Master for the certificate to be signed just after the ballot has been taken.

If a candidate for initiation[8] is unable to make the declaration on the second page of the Registration Form, covering such matters as convictions and disciplinary action by professional tribunals, he is obliged to delete the appropriate paragraph(s) or sub-paragraph(s) and provide a written explanation of the circumstances which prevent him from making an unqualified declaration. The form must then be sent to the Metropolitan, Provincial or District Grand Secretary to obtain a certificate that (if it is the case) the matters disclosed do not constitute a bar to the candidate being initiated. A Metropolitan, Provincial or District Grand Master has delegated authority to grant (but not to refuse) a certificate in certain limited circumstances, but in all other cases the certificate may be granted only by the Grand Secretary, thus ensuring consistency of approach throughout the Constitution.

If a certificate is refused, the Lodge into which the candidate seeks admission may resolve to challenge the Grand Secretary's refusal under Rule 164(a)(ii) by seeking a ruling under Rule 184. The requirement for certification has been in existence only since 1998, but it may be significant that so far there have been relatively few refusals and no challenges. This is not meant to imply infallibility on the part of the Grand Secretary, but rather that the requirement for certification has had its desired effect and deterred potential proposers and seconders from supporting unsuitable candidates.

Finally, the Secretary must also complete and sign the certificate on the last page of the form before sending the form (via the Metropolitan, Provincial or District Grand Secretary, if so required) to the Grand Secretary for registration.

Centenaries and Bi-Centenaries

If a Lodge is about to celebrate its Centenary or Bi-Centenary, the Grand Secretary will normally write to the Metropolitan, Provincial or District Grand Secretary inviting the Lodge to submit an enquiry as to whether and, if so, what evidence is required to support a Petition for a Centenary or Bi-Centenary Warrant. The relevant Rule is 252:

---

8   Or for joining or rejoining after a period as an unattached Mason.

"252. (a) Application for permission to wear a Centenary Jewel is to be made by petition or memorial to the Grand Master, in which memorial or petition the necessary particulars as to the origin and regular working of the Lodge are to be given, as well as proof of its uninterrupted existence for one hundred years.

"(b) Application for permission to attach a Bi-Centenary Bar to the ribbon of the Centenary Jewel must be similarly made and proof of two hundred years of uninterrupted existence established."

The Rule goes on to identify the jewel and bar (Plate No. 59) and those who are entitled to wear it.

It will be noted that a Lodge must be able to establish not only its origin (rarely a difficult thing to do) but also that it has worked regularly and has had uninterrupted existence for one hundred, or two hundred, years, as the case may be. In general, in order to establish the latter, the Lodge must show that it has not rendered itself at any time liable to be erased under Rule 189 (*i.e.* failed to meet for a whole year). If a Lodge has an interruption in its working, "the counter is reset to zero" and the Centenary then falls to be calculated from the date the Lodge resumed working; it is not a matter of merely delaying the Centenary by the length of the break. The Grand Master has, however, discretion to disregard a temporary break if he is satisfied that a Lodge has made every effort to hold meetings (though without success) or that it has been prevented from meeting by *force majeure*.

An enquiry will generally result in the answer that the records of the Grand Lodge establish continuity of working and that no further evidence is required. In a minority of cases possible gaps in working will be identified and evidence requested.

It might be thought that the possession of a Centenary Warrant would obviate the need for a Lodge approaching its Bi-Centenary to establish uninterrupted working during its first hundred years. Successive Grand Registrars, however, have advised over many years that the full two hundred years must be investigated afresh. There is no doubt that a hundred years or so ago, the Grand Lodge's records had not been arranged in such good order as they have been subsequently and that claims of a hundred years' uninterrupted working were less rigorously investigated than is now the case. In consequence a Centenary Warrant is treated as being conclusive only of those facts stated in it. Thus such a Warrant that recites (as is the invariable modern wording) uninterrupted existence for one hundred years is treated as conclusive evidence for that first hundred years,[9] whereas one that merely recites that the Lodge had attained the Centenary of its existence is treated as evidence only of one hundred years' *existence*, not of *uninterrupted* existence for that period. It is an interesting psychological phenomenon that some Lodges accept with relative equanimity the fact that because of a break in working during the first hundred years they are not, on this test, entitled to a Bi-Centenary Warrant, while others – and often their Provincial Grand Masters – become remarkably excited by a refusal. Does it matter if a Lodge is allowed a Bi-Centenary Warrant if it has a break in working in its first hundred years which would be sufficient to deny it a Centenary Warrant today? Alternatively, does it really detract from a Lodge's achievement in having existed for two hundred years that it cannot be granted a Warrant reciting (which is not the case) that it has worked without interruption for the whole of that period?

---

9   On the basis that the Grand Master must be presumed from such wording to have exercised his discretion to disregard such temporary break(s) in working, if any, as might have existed.

Part II

OUTSIDE THE LODGE

12

BEHAVIOUR IN THE BAR

Here's a Health to an Accepted Mason
The Enter'd 'Prentice's Song

This chapter will be a short one, since a far less formal atmosphere prevails during the drinking time before dinner than in either the meeting that precedes, or the meal that follows, it. The fact, however, that this part of the evening is more relaxed does not mean that anything goes.

The days are long gone, thank goodness, when a junior Brother would not dream of speaking to a Grand Officer or even a Provincial Grand Officer unless spoken to by him first. Nonetheless, there are occasions when diffidence is called for. An official visitor should be treated with greater deference than the senior Brethren of the Lodge with whom a junior Brother may, over time, have achieved a degree of familiarity. The Provincial Grand Master or another "chain" will almost always be accompanied by a Director of Ceremonies who will act as a buffer. It may be the latter, or it may be the Master or Secretary of the Lodge, who will introduce the members of the Lodge to him at the reception. It is likely that such Brethren will address him as "sir", and others should follow their example. However affable and approachable the Provincial Rulers may appear to be, it is not appropriate on an official visit to address them as "Mike" or "Bob" or "Ron" (if those should be their names).

Much the same will apply in the case of a Brother sent to represent the Provincial Grand Master, even though he may well not be accompanied by a Director of Ceremonies and will therefore appear to be more accessible.

It should go without saying that it is bad manners to back any official visitor (or, for that matter, any other senior Brother) into a corner or attempt to monopolise him (particularly if you are a visitor yourself[1]), though in the case of a "chain" his Director of Ceremonies is likely to be experienced in prising away those who show limpet-like tendencies. In particular, the bar is not the place to tell the Provincial Grand Master or his team what you think is wrong with Masonry, or your other ideas about it, however good they may be. If you feel that you do have something useful to say, tell him that you have some ideas that you would like to discuss with him or one of his team, listen to what he has to say about whom you should talk to, and leave him free to circulate among the other Brethren.

It is becoming common during the drinks before dinner for the Stewards or others to circulate among the Brethren, selling tickets for the raffle if one is to be held in conjunction with the after-proceedings. Such a raffle, generally using cloakroom tickets, constitutes a small lottery incidental to an exempt entertainment, and is lawful so long as the draw is made in the course of the evening and the whole proceeds of the evening (including the proceeds of the lottery) after deducting necessary expenses are devoted to purposes other than private gain. In December 1994 the Grand Lodge adopted a Report of the Board of General Purposes on the subject of lotteries, which made it clear that:

(a) a lottery with a Masonic character should, in general, be used to raise money only for charity, other benevolent purposes, or some other specific object not directed to private gain, and that no form of lottery should in any circumstances be used to defray the general running expenses of a Lodge, Province or District; and

(b) it is essential that the purpose for which any such lottery is held is clearly stated to anyone to whom tickets are offered for sale.

Whilst it is not actually unlawful to discount tickets (*e.g.* £1 per ticket; 5 tickets for £4) in such a raffle (though it is illegal for other classes of lottery), it should be regarded as contrary to the spirit of Masonry that those who are able or willing to spend more money buying tickets than other Brethren (perhaps more impecunious than them) should thereby be able to secure better odds of winning a prize.

---

1 If you are a visitor, you should remember that the official visitor will wish to meet and talk to the members of the Lodge rather than the other guests.

In some Masonic Halls the use of the bar may not be restricted to the Lodges meeting there, and in many, after dinner, there may be wives waiting to drive their husbands home. Non-Masons on such occasions will gain their ideas of the Craft from the way they see Brethren behaving, and therefore rowdy or loutish behaviour should be avoided. In short, normal good manners should prevail.

13

PROTOCOL AND BEHAVIOUR AT DINNER

You may enjoy yourselves with innocent mirth, treating one another according to ability, but avoiding all excess, or forcing any brother to eat or drink beyond his inclination, or hindering him from going when his occasions call him, or doing or saying anything offensive, or that may forbid an easy and free conversation; for that would blast our harmony, and defeat our laudable purposes.

The Charges of a Free-Mason – VI. Of BEHAVIOUR
2. Behaviour, after the lodge is over, and the brethren not gone

Many Brethren take the view that the after-proceedings are an essential part of a Lodge's meeting. From an historical point of view they are undoubtedly right, since in the eighteenth century the ceremonies themselves were very short and much the greater part of the Lodge's work was carried on at table, in the form of Lectures worked in catechetical form, that is by way of question and answer.[1] Nowadays the esoteric element has disappeared from the dinner or lunch that follows (or occasionally precedes) a meeting, with the result that the meal differs from any other formal meal only in respect of the wine-taking and the nature of the toasts that are drunk at its conclusion.

Seating

Lodges vary greatly in the degree of formality observed in the seating of the Brethren at table. A traditional top table with the Master in the centre will have sprigs running down from it, and the Wardens seated at the end of the outer sprigs. In such cases Grand Officers and senior Provincial Grand Officers are likely to be seated to the

---

1   The Lectures survive to this day, and the test questions before Passing and Raising are drawn from the First and Second Lecture respectively.

right of the Master, with, generally, the Immediate Past Master and senior Officers of the Lodge to his left. The remaining Brethren are seated more or less hierarchically on the sprigs. Another, less formal, arrangement is a single table, with the Master in the middle of one of the long sides and the Wardens at either end, and the remaining Brethren simply filling up the remaining places as the fancy takes them. There are also various other possible arrangements, such as a series of round tables.

Current practice tends towards a less hierarchical arrangement, but in any Lodge there will be occasions when a greater measure of formality is required, and even on relatively ordinary occasions there are certain principles that must always be observed. Except in a very small number of Lodges, where long-standing custom is otherwise, an initiate is always seated to the immediate right of the Master. Unless there is an initiate (in which case he moves one place to the right) an official visitor is seated on the immediate right of the Master.

If an official visitor is accompanied by a Director of Ceremonies, the latter is generally seated on the top table, but *at least* one place away from him, so that the official visitor has another member of the Lodge (or, less desirably, a very senior visitor) on his right. The visitor's Director of Ceremonies may perfectly properly be seated either to the right or to the left of the Master, and wherever his personal rank dictates (provided that he remains on, or in easy reach of, the top table), but preferably beside the Lodge's Director of Ceremonies in case joint action should be called for during either the meal or the toasts.

If the occasion is a particularly formal one, the seating on the top table will have been settled in advance of the meeting and agreed with the Metropolitan, Provincial or District Grand Secretary and/or the Assistant Grand Secretary on behalf of the Grand Secretary. (The "Grand Lodge" protocol is that seating in the Lodge is for the Grand Director of Ceremonies, and seating at the meal for the Grand Secretary, to resolve.)

As was seen in Chapter 5 in relation to seating in Lodge, there are considerable local variations, and it is therefore impracticable in a work of this size and nature to do more than document the basic Grand Lodge practice, which is the subject of those local variations. The seating arrangement at the luncheon that follows each Quarterly Communication and at the Grand Festival, the dinner that follows the Annual Investiture, is based on a system of round tables and takes account of the factors that are peculiar to each such individual occasion; it does not therefore fall within the scope of this book.

Other than meetings of the Grand Lodge, there are two types of event at which "Grand Lodge rules" apply: the Installation of a new Metropolitan, Provincial or

District Grand Master, and the Bi-Centenary (or, more rarely, the Centenary) of a Private Lodge. For each type, the principle of "interleaving" senior hosts with guests is observed, at least so far as the centre of the top table is concerned.

Whether the meal precedes or follows the Installation of, for example, a new Provincial Grand Master, the latter presides with his Deputy and Assistant Provincial Grand Masters in alternate seats either side of him, separated by the Ruler carrying out the Installation and the visitors in descending order of seniority as in fig. 1.

Assistant Provincial Grand Master 4 – or 6th visiting Provincial Grand Master[2]
4th visiting Provincial Grand Master
Assistant Provincial Grand Master 2
2nd most senior visiting Provincial Grand Master
Deputy Provincial Grand Master
Ruler or other Installing Officer
◄ Provincial Grand Master
Senior visiting Provincial Grand Master
Assistant Provincial Grand Master 1
3rd visiting Provincial Grand Master
Assistant Provincial Grand Master 3
5th visiting Provincial Grand Master
Assistant Provincial Grand Master 5 – or 7th visiting Provincial Grand Master

---

fig. 1

This arrangement continues, seating the *visiting* Grand Officers either side alternately for as many places as the top table contains. It should be noted, however, that the Grand Director of Ceremonies (or acting Grand Director of Ceremonies) always has his Deputies seated next to him (to whichever side of the Provincial Grand Master they naturally fall), so that to the opposite side of the Provincial Grand Master an equivalent number of visiting Grand Officers will be seated in straight succession before the alternating pattern is resumed.

The increasing pace of life and other factors have brought about a significant change in the way that the Installation on the same day of a new Provincial Grand

---

2   Depending on how many Assistant Provincial Grand Masters there are in the particular Province.

Master and a new Grand Superintendent (a "double-header") is organised. Twenty years ago the Royal Arch ceremony would take place in the late morning, followed by a luncheon, and the Craft ceremony in the late afternoon, followed by a dinner. If the Province was a significant distance from London, this usually involved the "London team" in a two-night stay in the Province, with a consequent increased expense for the latter. Over the intervening years it has become almost the invariable practice for the Craft ceremony to take place in the afternoon, as soon as convenient after the conclusion of the luncheon, which is therefore of necessity a combined event. The arrangement works remarkably well, with a considerable saving in time and expense, but it calls for a significant modification to the seating plan to accommodate the senior members of the Province's Royal Arch hierarchy and those Grand Superintendents who are not also Provincial Grand Masters.

In essence, the Craft hierarchy of the Province is ranged to the right, and the Royal Arch hierarchy to the left, of the new Provincial Grand Master and Grand Superintendent.[3] The visiting Provincial Grand Masters are then interleaved with the Craft hierarchy and Grand Superintendents with the Royal Arch hierarchy (not forgetting that some of the Provincial Grand Masters are likely to be themselves "double-headers" and can therefore be deployed to either side of the chair).

A rather simpler (or at least less high-powered) arrangement, following the interleaving principle, is adopted at a Bi-Centenary. In its classic form (rarely met with since the creation of the Metropolitan Grand Lodge), members of the host Lodge alternate with the members of the official deputation[4] and other Grand Officers[5] as in fig 2.

There is no particular protocol about which members of the Lodge are seated where on the top table on such an occasion; sometimes a Lodge will select those who are highest in rank and sometimes those who have been members of the Lodge longest. Alternatively, the Lodge Secretary might be seated next to the Grand Secretary, and so on.

---

3 If a separate Provincial Grand Master and Grand Superintendent are being installed on the same day, the seating plan is varied by placing the Installing Officer in the centre of the top table, with the Provincial Grand Master on his right and the Grand Superintendent on his left.

4 Consisting of the guest of honour, the Grand Secretary (or substitute) to read the Bi-Centenary Warrant, the Grand Director of Ceremonies (or substitute), and the Grand Chaplain (or substitute) to deliver an Oration.

5 Unless he is a member of the official deputation, the preference of a Grand Officer, however senior, who is the personal guest of one of the members, to sit with his host should be respected.

> 5th most senior Grand Officer
> Senior member or Officer of the Lodge
> 3rd most senior Grand Officer
> Senior member or Officer of the Lodge
> Guest of honour
> ◄ Worshipful Master
> Immediate Past Master
> 2nd most senior Grand Officer
> Senior member or Officer of the Lodge
> 4th most senior Grand Officer
> Senior member or Officer of the Lodge

fig. 2

On almost every occasion nowadays the situation will be complicated by the presence of a Metropolitan or Provincial deputation, the members of which will also need to be interleaved with those on the top table. There will be no one absolutely correct arrangement of the Brethren, and any seating plan will represent a more or less successful compromise. Often the best that can be hoped for is that the correct relative ranking can be maintained within the Grand Lodge and the Metropolitan or Provincial deputations respectively, as in fig 3 overleaf.

Regalia at dinner

The days are long past when Brethren dined in regalia as a matter of course. Indeed, since waiting staff are very rarely, if ever, Masons, a dispensation is required under Rule 178 of the Book of Constitutions. Except for the very few Lodges which have been granted a general dispensation under the Rule, the only occasions nowadays at which regalia is regularly worn by all Brethren are the annual Festivals of the four main Masonic Charities (and not always then), following a dispensation from the Provincial Grand Master or, if a Province holds its Festival in London, the Metropolitan Grand Master. The Grand Master's advisers gave guidance to the Charities on the matter in 2003, the essence of which was that normally Craft regalia (full dress) should be worn, including the Royal Arch breast jewel (or Grand Superintendent's collarette), but not under any circumstances the regalia of any other Order; it was permissible to dispense with aprons, provided that this applied to *all* those attending, and it was not appropriate for only chains to be worn – those entitled to collars must wear them.

A limited exception exists for the wearing of the Hall Stone Jewel in Buckinghamshire (see Chapter 2).

Senior member or Officer of the Lodge
5th most senior Grand Officer
Assistant Metropolitan or Provincial Grand Master
Senior member or Officer of the Lodge
3rd most senior Grand Officer
Assistant Metropolitan or Provincial Grand Master
Senior member or Officer of the Lodge
Metropolitan or Provincial Grand Master
Guest of honour
◄ Worshipful Master
Immediate Past Master
Deputy Metropolitan or Provincial Grand Master
2nd most senior Grand Officer
Senior member or Officer of the Lodge
Assistant Metropolitan or Provincial Grand Master
4th most senior Grand Officer
Senior member or Officer of the Lodge
Assistant Metropolitan or Provincial Grand Master
6th most senior Grand Officer
Senior member or Officer of the Lodge

fig. 3

Grace

At a Grand Lodge dinner or luncheon, Grace is said by the Grand Chaplain or his Deputy. At the Installation of a Metropolitan, Provincial or District Grand Master, Grace may be said either by the Brother acting as Grand Chaplain, or by the Metropolitan, Provincial or District Grand Chaplain.

In a Private Lodge, Grace before dinner is almost invariably said, but after dinner it is often sung. When said, it is usually the duty of the Chaplain, if there is one, and if not, of the Master or someone nominated by him. Even at a Centenary or Bi-Centenary the Grand Lodge protocol is that it is the privilege of the Lodge's Chaplain to say Grace, unless he chooses to surrender it to the acting Grand Chaplain; this is, of course, subject to the usual local variations in practice. It should never be forgotten that every Grace directly or indirectly invokes the Deity, and it should therefore be couched in appropriately respectful terms. A formula such as "Heavenly Pa, ta" is therefore strongly to be deprecated. If the common formula, "For what we are about to receive may T.G.A.O.T.U. make us truly grateful and make us ever mindful of the needs of others," is felt to be too hackneyed, there are many published compilations of graces on which to draw.

The usual sung Grace after dinner is the *Laudi Spirituali*, and though the words should be familiar to most Masons, they are sufficiently often printed or rendered incorrectly to justify setting them out here:

> *For these and all Thy mercies given,*
> *We bless and praise Thy name, O Lord.*
> *May we receive them with thanksgiving,*
> *Ever trusting in Thy Word.*
> *To Thee alone be honour, glory*
> *Now and henceforth for evermore.*
>
> Amen.

The dinner

In the case of a Private Lodge, the Master and his Wardens are usually provided with gavels in order to gain the attention of the Brethren for Grace, wine-taking and, later, the toasts. None of them should ever surrender his gavel to the Immediate Past Master, Director of Ceremonies or anyone else, unless for some reason he is obliged to leave the dining room. It is rarely necessary to gavel particularly loudly, and the Master, in particular, should bear in mind that the Provincial Grand Master or other senior Brethren on his right may prefer not to be deafened by an excess of enthusiasm on his part. The Junior Warden should try to preserve the equal rhythm of the knocks and not, as sometimes happens when the Senior Warden has been "slow off the mark", gavel the moment the other has done so, in order to show that he at least is "on the ball"; such action is an implied criticism of his immediate senior and is to be deprecated.

As a matter of principle, except in a case of *genuine* emergency, the Master and Wardens should never, and the other Brethren (other than those who have duties to perform as, for example, the Director of Ceremonies or Stewards) hardly ever, leave their places until the end of the after-proceedings. In particular, it is gravely discourteous to wander around during the meal and speeches in order to engage in social chit-chat.

Just as mobile telephones should be switched off in Lodge, so they should be at dinner. The only legitimate exception is someone such as a consultant surgeon who might be called in a crisis; such a Brother should set the ring-tone to "vibrate" and leave the dining-room before answering the call. Even such a Brother should not initiate a telephone call. It is equally a breach of good manners to read or send text messages while at table. The same applies to other hand-held communication devices.

It is elementary good manners not to start eating before the Master does so, and for this reason it is desirable that the latter should, as soon as he and the more senior Brethren around him have been served, make at least a token cut into the course which has been placed before him, in order that other Brethren may start to eat.

Wine-taking

The Board of General Purposes has had occasion to comment on the practice of wine-taking:

> "The practice by the Master of 'taking wine' at dinner becomes detrimental to congenial conversation unless kept to a minimum, and should be confined to Brethren in their Masonic status. The Board wishes to emphasise that Masonry can be brought into disrepute unless the Master ensures that after-proceedings are conducted with decorum. Challenging and cross toasting should not be permitted."

That was in 1956 and over the intervening years the practice of challenging[6] has all but died out. The same cannot be said of wine-taking, which still persists – in some Lodges largely unabated. The Grand Lodge protocol when wine-taking is controlled by the Grand Director of Ceremonies or his deputy is:

(a) at the Grand Festival after the Annual Investiture: the Grand Master

---

6 Challenging was a form of individual wine-taking in which one Brother called on another to take wine with him. It was hierarchically based, in that no one might challenge someone senior to him but only those equal to or below him in the pecking order, with the Master immune from challenge by any Brother. Though primarily good-natured in intent, it could result in a junior Brother ending up drinking rather too much and eating rather too little. It had therefore the potential for abuse by a concerted campaign against one individual. It survives today almost entirely in the unexceptionable form of one Brother catching the eye of another and raising his glass to him, thereby inviting him to take wine. It is not to be confused with such private wine-takings as the Deputies' toast, drunk by the Deputy Grand Directors of Ceremonies when the Grand Director of Ceremonies sits down after the formal wine-takings have been concluded.

(or Pro Grand Master) with the Brethren whom he has earlier invested in their new ranks; the Grand Master with the Board of Grand Stewards; and the Grand Master with all (he kindly requesting that they remain seated)

(b) at the luncheon following a Quarterly Communication: the Pro Grand Master (or Grand Master) with the Brethren from overseas; and the Pro Grand Master (or Grand Master) with all (he kindly requesting that they remain seated)

(c) at the Installation of a new Provincial Grand Master: the new Provincial Grand Master with the Ruler; the new Provincial Grand Master with the other Provincial Grand Masters (or with the other Right Worshipful Brethren); the new Provincial Grand Master joining with the Ruler to take wine with all (they kindly requesting that the latter remain seated)

(d) at the Consecration of a new Lodge: the Worshipful Master with the Consecrating Officer; the Worshipful Master with the Founders; and the Worshipful Master joining with the Consecrating Officer to take wine with all (they kindly requesting that the latter remain seated).[7]

(e) at a Private Lodge when a Ruler visits: the Master with the Ruler; the Master with all (he kindly requesting that they remain seated); the Ruler with all (he also kindly requesting that they remain seated)

(f) at a Private Lodge when a Ruler visits and the Metropolitan, Provincial or District Grand Master is also present: the Master with the Ruler; the Master with the Metropolitan, Provincial or District Grand Master; the Master with all (he kindly requesting that they remain seated); the Ruler and the Metropolitan, Provincial or District Grand Master with all (they also kindly requesting that the latter remain seated).

In cases (e) and (f), there is scope for additional (but appropriate) wine-takings in accordance with the established custom of the Lodge, provided that the overall total is not more than six.

---

7 *Alternatively*, the Worshipful Master with all (he kindly requesting that they remain seated); and the Consecrating Officer with all (he also kindly requesting that they remain seated).

As in many other cases, the Grand Lodge protocol is subject to local variation in a Metropolitan Area, Province or District.

At an ordinary meeting of a Private Lodge, wine-taking is usually under the control of the Immediate Past Master or the Director of Ceremonies. Not every Lodge engages in the practice, but when it does there are certain basic principles that should be observed. First, wine-taking should be confined to the intervals between courses. Secondly, it is customary in most Lodges for the Master to start by taking wine with his Wardens, and to finish by taking wine with all (he kindly requesting that they remain seated). Thirdly, it is "poor form" to take wine with an individual or a group of Brethren who will later be the subject of a formal toast, for example, Grand Officers.[8] Thus it is appropriate for the Master to take wine with his personal guests (provided that there are other visitors present), but not with *all* the guests. Similarly, on the night of the Installation it may be legitimate to take wine with the Immediate Past Master – but not if he is the subject of a formal toast later. Fourthly, as pointed out by the Board of General Purposes, wine-taking should be confined to Brethren in their Masonic status, which really means their Craft status.[9]

Smoking

Smoking in a public building is now illegal in England and Wales and this extends to a Masonic Hall or a Club. There are, however, still substantial parts of the English Constitution where smoking is still permitted, and it is therefore appropriate to remind readers of the established practice as it was observed until recently in London and Provinces, namely that smoking was not permitted until after the toast to the Grand Master.

The toast list

Most Metropolitan,[10] Provincial and District Year Books contain a toast list for use by Lodges within the Metropolitan Area, Province or District. Such lists are not

---

8 Another – and worse – example perhaps even more commonly met with is: "The Worshipful Master will be pleased to take wine with the Initiate", compounded, more often than not, by the further announcement, "The Worshipful Master is sure that you will all wish to take wine with the Initiate."

9 Taking wine with "members of the Royal Arch" is a legitimate exception, though at least one Provincial Grand Master has let it be known that he does not wish this to happen if he is himself present.

10 For the current toast list within the Metropolitan Area of London see the Appendix.

absolutely mandatory, but should normally be adhered to, though many Lodges, particularly the older ones, may have minor variations of their own. It is not necessary to drink every toast, but if the list is to be shortened, the objective should be achieved by omitting items from it, but not by combining two toasts into a single one.[11] Some Lodges have been known to drink "The Queen and the Craft", followed by "The Rulers in the Craft, supreme and subordinate", but this is to be deprecated.

The current standard toast list is:

The Queen and the Craft

* * * * *

The Most Worshipful The Grand Master
His Royal Highness The Duke of Kent
KG, GCMG, GCVO, ADC

* * * * *

The Most Worshipful Pro Grand Master
Peter Geoffrey Lowndes

The Right Worshipful Deputy Grand Master
Jonathan Spence

The Right Worshipful Assistant Grand Master
David Kenneth Williamson

and the rest of the Grand Officers, Present and Past

* * * * *

---

11 The formula adopted for a very brief time in a number of London Lodges following the Inauguration of the Metropolitan Grand Lodge of London of "The Most Worshipful Pro Grand Master, the Most Hon. the Marquess of Northampton, *DL*; The Right Worshipful Deputy Grand Master, Iain Ross Bryce, *TD, DL*; The Right Worshipful Assistant Grand Master, David Kenneth Williamson; The Right Worshipful Metropolitan Grand Master, the Rt. Hon. Lord Millett, *PC*; and the rest of the Grand Officers, Present and Past" well illustrates this point; it is permissible to *pick*, but not to *mix*.

[Metropolitan, Provincial or District Toasts – see below]

* * * * *

The Worshipful Master

* * * * *

[The Immediate Past Master]

* * * * *

[The Initiate]

* * * * *

The Visitors

* * * * *

The Tyler's Toast

Principal toasts

The first toast is to "The Queen and the Craft". For very many years the Monarch and the Craft have been conjoined in this way, irrespective of whether the Monarch is a Freemason or not. It should be noted that the correct form is "The Queen and the Craft" and not "Her Majesty The Queen and the Craft". If the National Anthem is sung at this point, it should follow the proposal, but precede the drinking, of this toast (see the Report of the Board of General Purposes adopted by Grand Lodge in December 1985). It is desirable that the Master sets an example to the rest of the Brethren by standing firmly to attention while the National Anthem is sung (see Chapter 8).

Current practice is that the letters denoting Orders etc after the name of the Grand Master and others so entitled – the so-called "honorifics" – though they should be printed in full on a toast list, are never spoken in proposing the toast. In connection with this and the third toast it should be noted that only the Grand Master has a second "The" in his title ("The Most Worshipful The Grand Master", but "The Most Worshipful Pro Grand Master").

The third toast is a long one, and an inexperienced Master is too often to be heard trying to break it down into what appear to be its constituent parts. The toast is, however, to *all* those listed, *i.e.* the Pro (*not* Provincial) Grand Master, the Deputy Grand Master, the Assistant Grand Master and the rest of the Grand Officers present and past (*not* past and present). Brethren standing to drink this toast are often heard to murmur as they do so "Grand Lodge", but that is quite wrong; all present Masters and Wardens, together with subscribing Past Masters, of Lodges are members of *Grand Lodge*, but they are not the subject of this toast, which is to *Grand Officers*.

Metropolitan, Provincial or District toasts

The form of the Metropolitan, Provincial or District toasts is the subject of variation according to the custom of the Province etc. Either of the following is legitimate:

The Right Worshipful Provincial Grand Master
John Charles Smith

* * * * *

The Deputy Provincial Grand Master
Very Worshipful Brother Peter Charles Jones, PGSwdB

The Assistant Provincial Grand Master(s)
Worshipful Brother(s) [names], PSGD

and the rest of the Provincial Grand Officers, Present and Past

or

The Provincial Grand Master
Right Worshipful Brother John Charles Smith

* * * * *

The Deputy Provincial Grand Master
Very Worshipful Brother Peter Charles Jones, PGSwdB

The Assistant Provincial Grand Master(s)
Worshipful Brother(s) [names], PSGD

and the rest of the Provincial Grand Officers, Present and Past

It is suggested that the first is to be preferred since it matches the style of the second and third toasts. On the other hand, the style:

The Right Worshipful Provincial Grand Master
Right Worshipful Brother John Charles Smith

is to be avoided, since it duplicates the prefix, applying it both to the office and the individual; while

The Very Worshipful Deputy Provincial Grand Master
Peter Charles Jones, PGSwdB

The Worshipful Assistant Provincial Grand Master(s)
[names], PSGD

and the rest of the Provincial Grand Officers, Present and Past

is wrong, since the prefixes at this level attach to the *individual* and not to the *office* – and in the case of a newly appointed Deputy Provincial Grand Master who has not yet been promoted in Grand Rank the first line would have to be amended to "The Worshipful Deputy Provincial Grand Master".

When there is an interregnum in a Metropolitan Area, Province or District as a result of the death or retirement of the Metropolitan, Provincial or District Grand Master, the fourth toast is omitted from the list and the first line of the fifth toast is amended, for example, to "The Deputy Provincial Grand Master in Charge". It is wrong to drink a toast to the latter separately from the other Provincial Grand Officers, even if he is the Provincial Grand Master designate.

It has already been noted in Chapter 5 that in some Provinces the official toast list has been amended, as a matter of courtesy, to embrace Provincial Grand Officers etc, other than those of the Province concerned. If the practice is to be observed, it is suggested that the correct formula for this is "and the rest of the Provincial Grand Officers, Present and Past of this Province and other Provinces, District Grand Officers, Present and Past, and holders of Metropolitan and Overseas Ranks". As a matter of principle it is wrong outside London to refer specifically to Metropolitan Grand Officers, as these Brethren have no precedence as such, but are all holders of either Senior London Grand Rank or London Grand Rank.

Other toasts

The toast to the Worshipful Master calls for no comment beyond the obvious remark that if it falls to the Immediate Past Master to propose this toast at every meeting, he should not use all his ammunition at the Installation meeting, but should keep a sizeable amount of it in reserve for the remainder of the year.

The toast to the Immediate Past Master or to the Installing Master, if drunk at all, should be confined to the Installation Meeting.

The toast to the Initiate is sometimes accompanied by the singing of the *Entered 'Prentice's Song*. It should be noted that this song, unlike most of those encountered at dinner, is genuinely old; it appears, with its accompanying tune, in the first (1723) edition of James Anderson's Constitutions.

Not every Lodge drinks a toast to Absent Brethren, but in most Lodges where it is given it has no fixed place in the list of toasts and is frequently drunk at nine o'clock. The idea has grown up that it is drunk at that hour because the hands of the clock are then "on the square",[12] but the custom had its origin in the First World War, so that Brethren on active service in the trenches and elsewhere should know at that hour that their Brethren at home were remembering them. This toast may not be drunk as a formal toast before "The Queen and the Craft" and "The Most Worshipful The Grand Master" (see *Information for the Guidance of Members of the Craft*) and therefore in some Lodges when dinner is running late it is drunk at nine o'clock as a commemoration, without fire.

The Tyler's Toast is generally preceded by a double knock from the Master (*not* repeated by the Wardens). In these days, when it is by no means the universal custom for the Tyler to dine with the Lodge, this toast is often given by the Director of Ceremonies. The correct form of the toast is the words of the Charge at the conclusion of the Third Section of the First Lecture, namely: "All poor and distressed Masons, wherever dispersed over the face of earth and water, wishing them a speedy relief from all their sufferings, and a safe return to their native country, if they desire it."

Fire

This is not the place to dilate on the origins or the symbolism of Masonic Fire, as to which in any discussion there will usually be as many opinions as there are

---

12 If the dinner is running early or late, so that the toast cannot be drunk at nine o'clock, the Master will sometimes announce that somewhere in the world the hands of the clock are on the square by way of introduction to the toast.

participants. It will be sufficient to say that the tradition of giving fire after a toast is a long-standing one both in Freemasonry and other contexts.[13]

Any toast of a Masonic nature may be followed by fire, including the first toast, "The Queen and the Craft". Accordingly, if fire is to be given after one such toast, it should be given after every such toast. Conversely, if a toast is drunk that is not Masonic in nature, *e.g.* in my Mother Lodge, "The School", fire must not be given. Fire is not, however, obligatory after a Masonic toast, and it should not be given while non-Masonic waiters are in the dining-room, or at a "white table".

There are, as in many other matters, local variations in the manner (not to mention the speed) of the fire, and it is not the province of this book to lay down any "correct" way of giving it. It should always be remembered that fire is intended to be an additional way of *honouring* a toast, and care should be taken that it does not degenerate into a contest to see who can give it fastest. If the slow speed of Emulation is not to everyone's taste, the excessively fast tempo adopted in some Lodges is at least as objectionable.

Speeches

Masonic speech-making is not what it used to be – but then it never was! The notion of a golden age when every Mason who stood to make a speech was able to hold his listeners spellbound, playing on first one emotion then another, is as ludicrous as it is enticing. It is salutary to find in *Freemasonry and its Etiquette* (see the Preface) the author commenting, "A considerable amount of ridicule is cast upon the quality of post-prandial oratory." Perhaps speakers in former times were more given to pomposity and sententiousness, which may have concealed the paucity of their invention better than the plainer speaking in fashion today, but it is doubtful whether the quality of Masonic speech-making was ever much higher (or much lower) than it is now.

Most Masons are not natural orators – and have no need to be. Except on a special occasion, such as a significant anniversary, there is no call for a lengthy speech; all that is required is something simple, to the point and, above all, short. There are a few straightforward and important rules every Mason should keep in mind when he has a speech to make.

First, if he knows he will have to make a speech after dinner, he should spend a few minutes earlier in the day mapping out the points he needs to make in the

13 For example, The Honourable Artillery Company.

course of the speech. This will give him confidence. Only a practised speaker can safely stand up and speak without having first given careful thought to what he is going to say; an inexperienced speaker standing up without knowing the essential points he wishes to put across is virtually certain to make a poor speech, halting in its delivery and rambling in its content. The novice can do worse than write it out beforehand and, when the time comes, read out the few sentences which are likely to be sufficient to cover his theme.

Secondly, he should speak up, and avoid mumbling and the intrusive "um" and "er". Reading a prepared speech should help to avoid the intrusive "um" and "er" (but it may actually encourage mumbling).

Thirdly, if the speech has not been written out, the next rule is: Keep to the point and do not ramble.

Fourthly, it will often help to lighten a speech, particularly at the toast to the visitors, with a little humour. This, however, should be used carefully. A little wit, an elegant turn of phrase, even a pun, are all acceptable – even when the last is of the "home-groan" variety. A joke or story, however, is a different matter. These are, on the whole, better avoided altogether, for the simple reason that more junior Brethren are liable to gain the idea that telling a joke is *the* thing to do. This leads too easily to someone trying to cap an innocuous story with a slightly risqué one, and so on, over a period of perhaps several meetings, until the stories have degenerated beyond the merely risqué to the positively dirty. If Brethren feel the need to tell dubious stories – and sometimes they can be very funny indeed if told well – they should keep them for the bar – preferably after, rather than before, dinner. If a speaker must tell a story, it should have some relevance to the rest of the speech: too often a speaker will say something along the lines of "Before I sit down I must tell you a story I heard last week" and launch into a joke that, however amusing, has absolutely nothing to do with Freemasonry or its after-proceedings. This merely serves to reinforce the impression in a junior Brother that when he makes a speech he should tell a joke. While it is not absolutely wrong to tell a story as though it concerned oneself, it is decidedly "bad form" to "father" a story on another Brother present (*e.g.* "The Provincial Grand Secretary went into the bank last week and...").

And the last rule? Above all, keep it short. The best of speakers, by leaving his hearers wishing he had gone on longer, will only enhance his reputation.

"White tables"

I have already referred to "white table" meetings in Chapter 6. In 1995 the Board of General Purposes reported:

"… it has become increasingly common for Lodges to entertain wives and other non-Masons to dinner. The Board does not wish to discourage this practice – indeed many non-Masons were present at the meal at Earls Court which followed Grand Lodge's Quarterly Communication in June 1992 celebrating its 275th anniversary – but hopes that it will remain the exception rather than the rule, and will be confined to perhaps a single meeting in each year.

"In the light of this change the Board has re-examined the policy on the giving of Masonic toasts on such occasions. It has concluded that there is nothing inherently improper in drinking the health of individuals in their Masonic capacity even though non-Masons are present, particularly when the latter are so clearly aware of the fact that the meal follows a Masonic meeting.

"The Board accordingly hopes that Grand Lodge will endorse its recommendation that there is no objection to drinking Masonic toasts in the presence of non-Masons, provided that Brethren in the course of speeches avoid references to matters of Masonic ritual. For this reason it also recommends that 'fire' and the Tyler's toast, both of which have their origins in the Masonic Lectures, should not be given on such occasions, particularly as the latter might be seen to be divisive by its exclusion of non-Masons from its scope. The Board also considers it desirable that the number of toasts drunk should be kept within reasonable bounds, so that non-Masons are not overwhelmed or confused, and suggests that it should rarely be necessary for the list to be longer than 'The Queen and the Craft', 'The MW The Grand Master', 'The Provincial (or District) Grand Master', 'The Worshipful Master' and 'The Guests'."

Part III

AWAY FROM THE LODGE

14

CORRESPONDENCE

230. The Board shall conduct the correspondence between the Grand Lodge and its subordinate Lodges and Brethren and communications with Sister Grand Lodges and Brethren of eminence and distinction throughout the world.

Rule 230, Book of Constitutions

All Freemasons from time to time write letters to other Freemasons. The use of e-mail is rapidly becoming more widespread, but almost all of the considerations that apply to the written word apply with equal force to the electronic word (and often to communication by telephone).

The same principles of etiquette apply generally to Masonic as to other correspondence, some of which are mentioned briefly below, but there are some additional matters that need to be observed in Masonic correspondence.

It is perfectly proper (and some would regard it as desirable) to use Masonic designations in a letter to another Brother.[1] This does not, however, extend to the envelope in which a letter is sent. In 1968 the Board of General Purposes reported to the Grand Lodge:

"It has been brought to the attention of the Board that members of the Craft are embarrassed by being addressed on envelopes in Masonic form. Brethren are asked to note that, on an envelope, the Masonic prefix to a recipient's name should not be used, nor should abbreviated Masonic ranks be so shown after the name."

It might be thought that forty years on and with the modern emphasis on openness (see Chapter 16) these words would now be outmoded, but that is not the case: the Brother receiving the letter is entitled to have his privacy

---

1 For guidance on styles and titles see Chapter 11.

respected, and he may have good reasons for not wanting his membership of the Craft more widely known than is unavoidable.

There is a curious habit of mind which is displayed by some Brethren when engaging in Masonic correspondence. They appear to believe that provided a letter begins "Dear Brother..." and ends "Yours sincerely and fraternally" it is permissible to write anything, however hair-raising, in between. This is not so, and the ordinary canons of polite behaviour should always be observed.

It was once the almost invariable practice for the Master Elect of a Lodge to write, soon after his election, to those whom he had provisionally chosen as his Officers, inviting them to serve and expressing the hope that they would accept. A Brother receiving such an invitation would write to accept, or gracefully decline, the office, in either case usually wishing the Master Elect a happy and successful year as Master. As a custom this seems to be in terminal decline, but it is possible – and to be hoped – that the ease of communication by e-mail will give it a new lease of life.

I have mentioned the "bread and butter" letter in Chapter 7. The converse of such a letter is an invitation and the response to it. An informal invitation issued in a simple letter is answered by a simple letter. A formal invitation, on a printed card, such as:

> The Worshipful Master, Wardens and Brethren
> of the
> Nonesuch Lodge, No. 9999
> request the pleasure of the company of
> W Bro. J.C. Smith
> at the
> Installation of Bro. Peter Edward Jones as Master of the Lodge
> at Nonesuch Masonic Hall
> on Friday, 1st May, 2009 at 5.30 p.m.
>
> R.S.V.P.   Dinner 7.30 for 8 p.m.

is answered in a formal manner, in the third person, and following the wording of the invitation, but *without* breaking the reply into lines:

"W Bro. J.C. Smith thanks the Worshipful Master, Wardens and Brethren of the Nonesuch Lodge, No. 9999 for their kind invitation to the

Installation of Bro. Peter Edward Jones as Master of the Lodge at Nonesuch Masonic Hall on Friday, 1st May, 2009 at 5.30 p.m., and has much pleasure in accepting [or very much regrets that he is unable to accept]."

As such formal invitations, however, become rarer it is becoming increasingly common for them to be accompanied by a printed card or form obviating the need for a formal reply (and the challenges associated with it).

There are two conventions and one Rule of which Brethren should be aware. The Rule is Rule 17 which provides:

"No communication on any Masonic matter shall be made to the Grand Master, except through the Grand Secretary."

As the Pro Grand Master is the Grand Master's *alter ego*, the Rule applies with equal force to communications to him also. Rule 17 is frequently mirrored in the by-laws of a Province by a requirement that all communications for the Provincial Grand Master should be sent via the Provincial Grand Secretary.

The first convention concerns correspondence (and telephone communications) with Brethren of other jurisdictions. In December 2004 the Board of General Purposes reminded the Grand Lodge that:

"It is an established Masonic convention that Masonic correspondence outside the Lodges and membership of the United Grand Lodge of England should be conducted through the offices of the respective Grand Secretaries. It appears from correspondence in the Grand Secretary's office from his colleagues in other jurisdictions that this convention is being increasingly disregarded. The Board wishes to remind members of the Craft that all enquiries directed to other Grand Lodges should be sent to the Grand Secretary at Freemasons' Hall, London. This applies equally whether the correspondence is conducted through the medium of the post or by electronic means such as e-mail and facsimile transmission.

"Where in certain areas overseas there are, in addition to an English District Grand Lodge or a Group under a Grand Inspector, similar bodies under other jurisdictions no exception is taken to contact **on routine matters** through our District Grand Secretary or Grand Inspector."

This is not intended to restrict friendly communication between Brethren of different Constitutions who already know each other, but it does prohibit the forming of new connections without the involvement of the respective Grand Secretaries, and even when the Brethren concerned are already acquainted it requires formal communications (or communications on formal matters) to be conducted in accordance with the convention. By way of an example, if a Brother is about visit Italy on holiday or on business and wishes to find a Lodge to attend while he is there, he should contact the Grand Secretary's Office (see also below) to ascertain which is the correct (*i.e.* recognised) Masonic authority in that country. It may be possible at this stage to arrange a Lodge for him to visit, but the more common course is for him to make contact with the Italian Grand Secretary's office once he is in Italy and arrange an introduction to a Lodge. Once he has visited that Lodge, he does not need a further introduction to it from either Grand Secretary, and if he has exchanged addresses (real or e-mail) with one or two of the members he may perfectly properly correspond with them. If, however, he wishes at some later date to arrange a visit by the Italian Lodge to his English Lodge, or vice versa, this must be done through the respective Grand Secretaries, that being the standard – and formal – procedure for such matters.

The second convention, which is less firmly established as such, is that communications between Brethren in London, Provinces and Districts and the Grand Secretary are via their respective Metropolitan, Provincial or District Grand Secretaries. There are clearly occasions when this convention does not apply. An obvious example is the lodging of an appeal under Rule 185 against the decision of a Metropolitan, Provincial or District Grand Master. In most cases, however, it does apply, and a communication direct to the Grand Secretary is likely to be passed rapidly to the appropriate Metropolitan, Provincial or District Grand Secretary to deal with. This is not a deliberate policy on the part of the Grand Secretary and his staff to avoid having to answer correspondence; it is intended to make the most efficient use of the resources available to the Craft. A Provincial Grand Secretary, for example, will be familiar with most situations that might give rise to an enquiry to the Grand Secretary, but even more importantly he will know local conditions and may well know the Brethren involved. If an unusual situation has arisen in a Lodge and it seems unlikely that the Provincial Grand Secretary will know the answer, it is still only a sensible courtesy to let him know that a problem exists and to enlist his help in solving it. Regrettably, one reason for some Brethren writing direct to the

Grand Secretary is often that they have already received an answer they do not like from their Provincial Grand Secretary and hope for a "better" one from higher authority. In so doing they are not above presenting a carefully edited version of the facts on which they seek "advice", or at least suppressing from the Grand Secretary background information of which their Provincial Grand Secretary would naturally be aware.

15

ORDINARY LIFE

You are to act as becomes a moral and wise man; particularly not to let your family, friends, and neighbours, know the concerns of the lodge, &c., but wisely to consult your own honour, and that of your antient brotherhood, for reasons not to be mentioned here. You must also consult your health by not continuing together too late or too long from home after lodge hours are past; and by avoiding of gluttony or drunkenness, that your families be not neglected or injured, nor you disabled from working.

The Charges of a Free-Mason – VI. Of BEHAVIOUR
5. Behaviour at Home and in your Neighbourhood

Whether your Lodge meets only two or three times a year or every month, even if you belong to so many Lodges that you are out every night of the week, most of your life will be spent away from the Lodge. Being a Freemason is not a full-time occupation. This chapter is not intended to be a moralising sermon on exemplifying all the Masonic virtues in your everyday life, but just a brief summary of things that every Freemason should bear always in mind.

In June 1987 the Board of General Purposes reminded the Grand Lodge:

"It must be clearly understood by every member of the Craft that his membership does not in any way exempt him from his duty to meet his responsibilities to the society in which he lives. The Charge to the new Initiate calls on him to be exemplary in the discharge of his civil duties; this duty extends throughout his private, public, business or professional life. The principles of the Craft make it clear to him that his duty as a Freemason does not conflict with his duty as a citizen, but reinforces it." *(Information for the Guidance of Members of the Craft – "Freemasonry and Society".)*

Rule 179 provides: "As a citizen every Freemason has a duty not to engage in conduct which is contrary to the law of the land. As a Freemason he also has a duty not to engage in activity which may bring Freemasonry into disrepute." Those words were added in 1988, but the principle they embody was always implicit in Freemasonry. Fifty years ago a Freemason convicted of a crime of dishonesty or violence would almost certainly have resigned promptly from his Lodge or Lodges, and if he did not do so he would have been frozen out by his Brethren or excluded under Rule 181 (or its predecessors). Such a Brother remained a Freemason – though unattached – and liable to be subjected to Masonic disciplinary proceedings, but in practice such action was unnecessary and was very rarely taken.

Changes in society at large have brought about changes in Freemasonry in turn, and over the years it has been found necessary not only to make explicit a Freemason's duty to obey the law but also to impose disciplinary sanctions on those who do not. It is true that many Brethren convicted of criminal offences now choose to resign from the Craft (as opposed to their Lodges) under Rule 183A (an option that has been available to them only since the end of 1997), but they do so in many, if not most, cases to avoid disciplinary proceedings. It is a salutary comment that by far the greatest number of expulsions and suspensions imposed are for breaches of the first paragraph of Rule 179 and hardly any for purely Masonic offences. It is important to see this in perspective: such sanctions are necessary in order to preserve the good reputation of Freemasonry, but the number of occasions on which they have to be imposed is also, mercifully, small in proportion to the size of the Craft.

Just as criminal behaviour or professional misconduct damages (or has the potential to damage) the reputation of the Craft, so does anti-social or rowdy behaviour. It should not need saying that Brethren leaving a Masonic Hall in a residential area should avoid disturbing the neighbours; as in large things, so in small. All of us have the ability to damage the reputation of Freemasonry. Equally, however, we all have the ability to enhance it.

Every Freemason should remember, as he is frequently reminded, that he must not pursue his Masonic career at the expense of himself, his family and friends, or his work. It is easy at times to lose sight of the fact that a Mason who gives more money to Masonic Charities or more time to attending Lodge meetings (and the other calls of Freemasonry) than his circumstances really permit is not showing himself to be a good Freemason: he is showing himself to be a *bad* Freemason. His doing so may be due to ambition, or to pressure put on him by others in his Lodge because he "is not pulling his weight", but those applying such pressure are acting contrary to the principles of Freemasonry and deserve censure no less than him. It is the corollary that if a Brother succeeds in being respectable in life and useful to mankind he will be an ornament to Freemasonry even if his circumstances prevent him from attending his Lodge as often as he – or others – would wish.

One of the most difficult areas is the use – or alleged use – of Freemasonry for personal gain. It is not always easy to see where the dividing line should be drawn between what is permissible and what is not. In this context I remember the story (perhaps "fable" would be a better word) of the squire who was interviewing three applicants for the job of his coachman. He asked each of them how close he could drive his coach to the edge of a precipice. "Six inches," said the first; "Two inches," said the second; "Lord love you, Sir," said the third, "I'd never dream of driving anywhere near a precipice!" He got the job. In other words, if you have to debate with yourself (or others) whether something falls the right or the wrong side of a dividing line, it will almost certainly not be within the spirit of Freemasonry.

The vital question here is whether the disclosure that an individual is a Freemason generates business that would not otherwise have been secured. A great deal may turn on the nature of the goods or services being offered. Thus a manufacturer or retailer of Masonic regalia passes the test; so does a publisher of Masonic books and rituals – both are providing a necessary facility. On the other hand, a fishmonger who sets up business as "Square and Compasses Fish" fails the test, as his is a blatant pitch to secure the custom of Freemasons in a business that has no specific Masonic connection. Between the two extremes there are many gradations – and the edge of the precipice. One of the most insidious schemes that currently arise is that of the Brother (or his Company) who makes a pitch for the custom of Freemasons accompanied by a promise that for every unit sold a donation will be made to a Masonic Charity. There is nothing inherently novel in such schemes. Almost fifty years ago the Board of General Purposes reported:

"The attention of the Board has been drawn to the existence of what purport to be 'Masonic' Tours to other countries. The Board wishes to emphasize to the Craft that such Tours have no official sanction or standing and that circularization of Lodges or individuals by members of the Craft as such who are in anyway connected with Travel Agencies or Services must be deemed to be an attempt to make use of Masonry to secure professional, commercial or sectional advantages. The Board considers irrelevant any argument that such Tours are not conducted on a profit-making basis.

"The attention of the Board has been drawn also to the practice of inserting into advertisements or circulars direct quotations from, or references to, phrases of Masonic ritual which can hardly fail to convey to the initiated reader that they have been produced by Freemasons and are designed to catch the eye of Freemasons. The Board draws the clear inference from such productions that the authors are making use of their Masonic capacity to attract custom or support.

"The Board hopes that it will have the support of Grand Lodge in putting a stop to practices which, in its opinion, are liable to bring Masonry into disrepute, and which, in its opinion, contravene the ruling given by Grand Lodge as recently as June, 1956, on the subject of advertising." (March 1961)

On the other hand, no censure would attach to a Brother carrying on business as a travel agent who, at the specific and unsolicited request of, for example, his Provincial Grand Master arranged a "Masonic" Tour to the Holy Land for members of the Province and their wives or partners.

There are various ways to which Brethren resort of deliberately drawing attention, with a greater or lesser degree of subtlety, to their Masonic membership. If the object is personal gain or advancement none of them are acceptable, and even when the motive is innocent they are not necessarily "good form". Wearing the Craft tie or another recognisably Masonic tie to a job interview is both unacceptable and likely to be self-defeating, and wearing such a tie when not at a meeting can be suspect. In my younger days, when a plain black tie was the most usual tie for general Masonic wear, Brethren would commonly not wear it during the day, when it could be a "give-away", and only change into it just before a meeting. An identifiably Masonic case is another "give-away". So too are cuff-links, tie pins, rings, etc with a square-and-compasses or other Masonic design, though these have tended to be regarded as primarily a matter of taste or discretion:

"There has, in addition, been a proliferation in recent years of items of personal Masonic jewellery such as Masonic charms on watch chains, tie pins, lapel buttons and cuff-links. The wearing of such items is primarily a matter for discretion, but the Board hopes that Brethren will recognise that using them as items of personal adornment might in some circumstances be interpreted as seeking to use Masonic membership for personal advantage." (Extract from a letter to all Lodge Secretaries from the Grand Secretary in September 1991.)

Lapel badges (usually relating to Orders beyond the Craft) tend to be regarded as matters of "taste or discretion" but, except for the fact that they are usually concealed beneath a collar and are for that reason turned a blind eye to, they fall clearly within the scope of Rule 241 if worn in Lodge. They are not only a means of advertising Masonic membership in ordinary life (and therefore objectionable on that score) but are also a means of drawing attention to, and thereby potentially recruiting members for, other Masonic Orders, as to the desirability of which the reader is entitled to arrive at his own views.

Finally, those involved in public life need to be particularly alive to the risk of accusations of Masonic influence, as the Board of General Purposes pointed out in December 1989:

"A recent investigation by the Local Ombudsman suggests that some Brethren may not have fully understood the implications of what is said about declarations of interest in the Board's leaflet 'Freemasonry and Society', which was re-issued in a revised form and with Grand Lodge's approval in September 1988.

"In local government, as in many walks of life, the pecuniary interests of those involved in making decisions must be disclosed. Other interests (which may include Freemasonry) may also be appropriate for disclosure. Such interests should be disclosed if they are likely to have a bearing on the matter under discussion or on relationships with any of the people concerned. The disclosure need not be specific (e.g. 'I declare an interest' would be enough). After disclosure of an interest, the standing orders or customs of the committee or council, etc., will govern further participation in making the decision concerned.

"Brethren who may be involved in local government or where similar rules apply should consider the foregoing advice against the background of the leaflet 'Freemasonry and Society'. If difficulties arise, the Grand Secretary should be consulted (through the Provincial and District Grand Secretaries if appropriate)." (*Information for the Guidance of Members of the Craft* – "Declarations of Interest".)

16

OPENNESS

Forcibly impress upon them the dignity and high importance of Masonry;
seriously admonish them never to disgrace it; charge them to practise out of
the Lodge those duties they have been taught in it; and by virtuous, amiable
and discreet conduct to prove to the World the happy and beneficial effects
of our ancient institution...

Address to the Master, Ceremony of Installation

The reclusive image that Freemasonry had as little as thirty years ago was,
relatively speaking, a recent development. Masons have a long history of
appearing in public, often in regalia, going right back into the eighteenth century,
as the satirical print of "The Procession of the Scald Miserable Masons" testifies.

Although the sort of derision encouraged by that caricature led to the
restriction on indiscriminate processions of Freemasons in regalia, which now
survives in Rule 178 and Number 13 of the Summary of the Antient Charges
read to the Master Elect at his Installation, there is a long history of Freemasons
appearing in regalia in public on duly authorised occasions to lay foundation
stones etc. There was also regular reporting in the press of Masonic events, large
and small.

During the Second World War, the general ethos of "careless talk costs lives"
(coupled with a shortage of newsprint) led to an increased reticence about
Freemasonry as well as about many other things, and that culture prevailed until
the 1980s. In 1984, however, the Grand Master opened a permanent exhibition
on Freemasonry and its history in what was then known as the Library and
Museum Extension (and, following the closure of the exhibition after some
twenty years, has recently been renamed the Prince Regent Room). At the same
time members of the public started to be encouraged to walk into Freemasons'
Hall "off the street", not only to visit the exhibition but also to join one of the

hourly tours of the Grand Temple and other principal rooms in this gem of *art deco* architecture.

This was the beginning of an era of renewed openness, and of a firm policy of moving to rebut unfavourable coverage of Freemasonry in the press, instead of the previous policy of "no comment". Open days began to be held in Masonic Halls throughout the country, and the 275th anniversary of the Grand Lodge was celebrated at its Quarterly Communication on 10 June 1992, held at Earls Court, with an attendance of some eleven and a half thousand Freemasons of this Constitution and representatives of 88 other Grand Lodges, as well as a number of non-Masons who were either family and friends of Freemasons or representatives of the media. Ten years later, in 2002, a highly successful "Freemasonry in the Community" week was held, with events happening almost simultaneously all around England and Wales, resulting in some excellent local publicity, though little at national level. One of the highlights of this co-ordinated event was a service in St. Paul's Cathedral, at which the Dean of St. Paul's, the Very Reverend John Moses, not himself a Freemason, preached an inspirational sermon. In the course of the ten years that separated those two events, in 1999, the Board of General Purposes had reported:

"Every Mason is free to reveal his own Masonic membership, except when it might appear that business, professional or personal advantage is thereby being sought for himself or another. The Board believes that Brethren should be encouraged to acknowledge their membership with pride." (*Information for the Guidance of Members of the Craft* – "Masonic Secrets".)

In consequence of this change in outlook, Brethren have been far more ready to disclose the fact that they are Masons and to speak about Freemasonry to their friends and sometimes to a wider circle. Not all of this has necessarily been well judged on their part. Running a successful open day, or a presentation to non-Masons before a "white table", demands far more preparation and background knowledge than many Freemasons appreciate. In the case of an open day at a Masonic Hall it is likely that the Provincial Information Officer will be closely involved as a matter of course, but those organising a "white table" would do well to seek advice from the Provincial authorities. Altogether in a different league, however, is the giving of interviews to the media, particularly the broadcast media. In September 2005 the Board of General Purposes reported to the Grand Lodge:

"There has recently been a revival in interest in Freemasonry on the part of the broadcast media. The Board believes it timely to remind Brethren of the general advice given on this subject on previous occasions. Whilst it has no desire to prevent Brethren from voicing their views, the Board believes that participation, at both the national and local levels, in broadcast debates on Freemasonry is best left to spokesmen who have the background knowledge and experience to participate in such events, and, preferably, have been duly authorised in advance. Any Brother who is approached to take part in a broadcast should seek guidance either from the Communications Department at Freemasons' Hall or the Information Officer appointed by his Metropolitan, Provincial or District Grand Master. It follows also that Brethren, other than those authorised, should not voluntarily approach the media to solicit coverage." (*Information for the Guidance of Members of the Craft* – "Freemasonry and the Media".)

* * * * *

It is inevitable that the content of this and the previous chapter will overlap to some extent, and in some cases I have been unsure whether to include a particular topic under "Ordinary Life" or "Openness". To draw together the threads of both, and to close, here are some "do's" and "don'ts":

- In circumstances where there can be no suspicion that you are trying to use Freemasonry for your own advancement, *do* feel free to acknowledge your membership of the Craft (*e.g.* by listing it as a hobby or interest in a publication such as *Who's Who*).

- *Don't* "out" other Freemasons unless it is certain that they will not object or be embarrassed.

- *Don't* wear items of Masonic jewellery on inappropriate occasions.

- *Don't* volunteer the fact that you are a Freemason in a context where there is no reason for you to do so – such an action is liable to be misconstrued by Mason and non-Mason alike.

- If you are asked, in either a merely neutral or a positively hostile way, whether you are a Freemason, *don't* say that you are not. If you don't want to answer the question, say that you don't see why you should answer it; and if the other person intimates that he or she will take that as a "Yes", tell him or her directly that that is not what you said and that he or she is making an assumption.

- *Don't* brag about how important you are in Freemasonry; those who really are, don't (and don't need to); and if you are not, the likelihood is that you will sooner or later find that you have brought embarrassment or even ridicule upon yourself.

- However tempting it may be to do so, *don't* carry a Masonic quarrel into the public domain; you are likely to do the Craft – and yourself – at least as much harm as you do the other party. ("He who is intent on vengeance should first dig *two* graves.") Above all, don't report a Brother to his professional or trade regulatory body just because you are offended by the way he has behaved in a Masonic context. The regulator is concerned with his professional conduct and is likely to be unable to take any cognisance of the matter; all that you will have done is bring Freemasonry into disrepute.

Appendix

METROPOLITAN GRAND LODGE OF LONDON

TABLE OF APPOINTMENTS

Deputy Metropolitan Grand Master
6 Assistant Metropolitan Grand Masters

SLGR   LGR

Metropolitan
- Grand Inspectors – 21
- Senior Grand Warden
- Junior Grand Warden
- Grand Chaplain
- Grand Treasurer – elected
- Grand Registrar
- Grand Secretary
- Grand Director of Ceremonies
- Grand Sword Bearer
- Grand Superintendent of Works
- Deputy Grand Chaplain
- Deputy Grand Registrar
- Deputy Grand Secretary
- Deputy Grand Directors of
  Ceremonies – 3
- Deputy Grand Sword Bearer
- Grand Almoner
- Grand Charity Steward
- Grand Mentor
- Grand Orator

Metropolitan
- Grand Deacons – 10
- Assistant Grand Chaplain
- Assistant Grand Registrar
- Assistant Grand Secretary
- Assistant Grand Directors of
  Ceremonies – 10
- Grand Organist
- Grand Standard Bearers – 5
- Deputy Grand Organist
- Grand Pursuivant
- Assistant Grand Pursuivant
- Grand Stewards – 20
- Grand Tyler

TOAST LIST

The Queen and the Craft

—

The Most Worshipful The Grand Master
His Royal Highness The Duke of Kent, KG, GCMG, GCVO, ADC[1]

—

The Most Worshipful Pro Grand Master
Peter Geoffrey Lowndes

—

The Right Worshipful Deputy Grand Master
Jonathan Spence

—

The Right Worshipful Assistant Grand Master
David Kenneth Williamson

—

And the rest of the Grand Officers, Present and Past[2]

—

The Right Worshipful Metropolitan Grand Master
Russell John Race, DL

—

The Deputy Metropolitan Grand Master
R.W. Bro Michael Ward, PJGW

—

The Assistant Metropolitan Grand Masters
The Metropolitan Grand Inspectors

—

The Officers of Metropolitan Grand Lodge
Other holders of SLGR, LGR and LR
{ and Officers of Provincial and District Grand Lodges, Present and Past }[3]

—

The Worshipful Master

—

The IPM or Installing Master
(on Installation night)

—

The Initiate or Initiates (if any)

—

The Visitors (if any)

—

The Tyler's Toast

[1]. *The Honorifics (KG etc) should be omitted when proposing this toast*
[2]. *There need not always be a reply to this toast*
[3]. *{} Optional*

INDEX

NOTES